Pipe
Organ
Registration

Pipe Organ
Registration

JACK C. GOODE

𝄞

abingdon press

nashville • new york

A Ma Bien Aimée

Foreword

This book is first and foremost a teaching manual, designed to introduce progressively the problems of registration and to provide material for study, along with assignments to aid the student in developing his capacity to cope with varied situations. Subtitles are provided to make it easy for a teacher to assign various portions of the chapters dealing with the different schools of organ playing as they may apply to literature used at any given period in the first two or three years of study. It is the author's philosophy that the most satisfying performance of any music is that which comes closest to reproducing it as heard by the composer. Admittedly not every organist will agree with this premise. Even to those of differing persuasion, however, the material on the various schools of organ playing will be useful in providing historical background, a facet of study not to be overlooked in any field of endeavor where significant information exists.

Basic discussion of forms is provided to clarify their bearing on the selection of appropriate registration. As a guide to the study of great literature, specifications of significant instruments from different countries and built in different centuries are provided, as well as a short outline of the history of the organ.

Detailed registrational suggestions are given for a few selected works. Realizing that an instructor will be explicit in choice of registers at the student's disposal, the author has furnished a model for study useful (a) to students who lack adequate instruments, that they may know something of relatively ideal procedures, and (b) to save time for the instructor in lessons. The student will learn from his effort, and needed adjustments can easily be made by his instructor. No works chosen for this purpose are considered less than good literature. The author realizes that some of the pieces presented in this

7

analytical manner can be registered musically in more than one way.

The dictionary of organ stops does not attempt to provide detailed technical information but rather a source of data to help the student as he studies various organs and organ specifications, new and old. In keeping with this purpose, some organ stops now considered obsolete have been included.

There are chapters on articulation, hymn accompaniments, vocal and choral accompaniments. These features make the text valuable in organ pedagogy courses as well as for teaching beginners. It is the hope of the author that he has provided here an aid to the individual teacher and student alike and greatly reduced the amount of time that must be taken from weekly lessons for discussion and development of the varied problems of registration involved in great organ literature. Realizing that the building in which each organ is housed forms an integral part of the instrument, the author feels that only an experienced instructor can help the student as he strives to adjust to the problems peculiar to each organ he must play.

The author wishes to acknowledge the generous advice, help, and encouragement of numerous friends and associates. Among these are Corliss R. Arnold, William H. Barnes, Malcolm D. Benson, Barrett L. Spach, Robert Stebbins, Frederick Swann, and Robert Weber. And last but not least, he wishes to express appreciation of his wife's infinite patience and her assistance in translations without which this book would not have been possible.

—JACK C. GOODE

Suggestions for the Use of This Book

The basic material of the first nine chapters can be assigned early in the student's study of the organ. The instructor may wish to make minor alterations in suggested procedures dealing with ensemble building, but the basic plan presented will quickly develop familiarity with the quality and dynamic levels of all stops. Peculiarities of ensemble building that reflect varied schools and periods are obviously too complex to be assimilated except in very slow stages.

Chap. 10 can be used at any appropriate time to clarify for the student the tonal structure of any small instrument which employs unification or duplexing.

Chap. 11 is not intended as an end in itself but as a *means* of learning to analyze the resources of any given organ and, through experience, to shorten the time the student will require to handle any new organ he may encounter. It also provides a check on the degree of assimilation of the material of the first nine chapters.

Chap. 12 is to be used for reference purposes as the student begins to study organs of various countries.

Chaps. 13 and 14 will prove useful late in the first year of study as the student begins to deal with romantic music such as the Mendelssohn sonatas.

The material of Chaps. 15 through 21 is obviously designed to shed light on a wide variety of literature. The Italian organ is discussed first, due to its simplicity, but the material of Chap. 18 will likely be of use relatively early in the first year of study. Beginning in the section entitled "Bach's Organ" is entirely feasible, and the direct bearing of its material on literature in use will lend relevancy and interest for the student. The general "Rules for the

Performance of the Music of Bach" will bear much study, and specific works discussed may be incorporated into the student's routine with a resulting rapid assimilation of important principles. Parts of the chapter obviously deal with advanced literature and can be used at any appropriate time.

Chap. 24 can be used for reference almost from the first day of study. It is suggested that the first three rules given be learned at the outset and exceptions studied as they may be encountered.

Contents

1

INTRODUCTION TO THE CONSOLE AND ITS STOPS

As a beginning organ student seated at the organ console, you face a battery of controls that is likely to intrigue and baffle you. And yet, by approaching in simple stages the problems of handling this seemingly huge king of instruments, you will quickly assimilate basic essentials and, in time, become the master of its many mysteries. The first things you need to understand are the names and uses of the keyboards (manuals).

The Manuals

Most pipe organs have only two or three keyboards, as well as a pedal board designed to be played by the feet of the organist. The pedal board and the manuals each control a division or "organ" made up of ranks (rows) of pipes in separate chambers.[1] Each division contains a variety of stops or voices of different pitches; these stops also have varied tone colors. The two-manual organ has both Great and Swell divisions. In a three-manual organ the Choir division is

[1] Sometimes divisions are unenclosed in order that they can speak directly into the building where they stand.

usually played from the lowest manual (I), and above it are the Great (II) and Swell (III) manuals. In England and America the manuals are named and numbered as follows: [2]

Division Name	Two-Manual	Three-Manual	Four-Manual
Solo (Bombarde)			IV
Swell	II	III	III
Great	I	II	II
Choir (Positiv)		I	I

Some organs have Echo or Antiphonal divisions, or "floating" [3] Positiv or String divisions.

The purpose of the various manuals is to afford the opportunity of contrasted levels of volume or types of ensemble or to allow contrasts in solo and accompaniment textures.

Stops—Their Nomenclatures

The stop tablets or draw-knobs of the console control the ranks of pipes, bringing them into play or keeping them silent until they are needed. Their nomenclatures describe the quality and pitch of the various stops (individual "voices") in the different organs. The basic groups of organ stops fall into two categories and four families:

1. diapasons
2. flutes   FLUES (or labials)
3. strings

4. reeds   REEDS (or linguals)
    solo reeds (clarinet)
    ensemble reeds (trumpet)

Further description of these "families" of stops will help you familiarize yourself with their individual qualities; for the present

[2] The system of numbering used in France and Germany dictates that Manual I be the Great regardless of whether it is placed as the lowest or the second manual; other manuals are then numbered from the bottom upward, e.g., II (Rückpositiv or Positif) and III (Oberwerk or Récit).
[3] Playable from various manuals.

time the flues comprising the first category of stops are discussed in some detail.

Diapasons

The diapason is considered the true foundation tone of the organ, a sound peculiar to the instrument. Its importance is seen in the fact that the name is a Greek word meaning "from the first to the last note." Some equivalents are (a) G.[4] prinzipal, (b) I. principal, (c) F. montre (meaning show or display pipes). With its various ranks this family is the most important of the organ. Diapason tone lies somewhere between flute and string tone, but is completely individual. It combines ample fundamental tone with good harmonic development. The family includes the diapasons 16′ and 8′ (principal, violin diapason, geigen principal); octave (8′ in pedal, 4′ in manual divisions); twelfth; fifteenth; and various compound stops known as mixtures which we shall discuss in more detail later.

Flutes

Flutes are flue pipes with high-cut mouths and relatively low harmonic development, although there is an amazing variety of flutes with considerable variation in their construction. They are made of wood or metal and may be (a) open, (b) stopped, or (c) partially stopped. Various hybrid tones result from the different treatment given to the caps of pipes.

Stopping a pipe has the effect of making it sound an octave lower than it would sound if open. This principle has been employed in organ design not simply for economy purposes but for the reason that it creates new and distinctive voices.

The "harmonic" flute is one which, on the other hand, has been constructed twice the length of the pitch desired and "overblown" to produce its octave, the speaking of this particular harmonic being facilitated through the placing of a hole in the side of the pipe at its half-length (where that partial or overtone normally occurs). Some types of *stopped flutes* are: bourdon (wood), cor de nuit,

---

[4] Key to abbreviations to be used throughout this text: L-Latin, G-German, D-Dutch, F-French, S-Spanish, I-Italian, E-English, Gk-Greek. German nouns, usually capitalized, are given in lowercase for ease in reading.

doppelflöte (double flute having two mouths on opposite sides), gedeckt (or gedackt), lieblichflöte (or lieblichgedeckt), nason flute (with pronounced twelfth), quintaton (quintadena, metal flute with strong twelfth), stopped diapason (or stopped flute).

Some *open flutes* are: clarabella, concert flute, hohlflöte, major flute, melodia, orchestral flute (or flauto traverso), blockflöte, flûte ouverte, harmonic flute, nachthorn, sifflöte, spitzflöte (tapered with narrow top and having an audible seventeenth; also called flûte conique), waldflöte.

Strings

Strings are the flues with highest harmonic development. They are generally of metal, relatively narrow, and have special mouth treatment to bring about their unique qualities. Strings sometimes use rollers or harmonic bridges to help facilitate their speech. Some common members of the string family are gamba, salicet, salicional, viola,[5] viole de gambe, viole d'orchestre, violina, violone, violoncello, viola pomposa. Strings may be orchestral (imitative) in character or foundational (stops that blend well in ensemble).

Stops—Their Pitches

You are doubtless curious about the numbers to be found on all stop tablets[6]; these define the pitches of the various ranks of pipes. For example, a flute 8′ is a flute sounding at *basic* pitch or at the same pitch as that heard when playing a given note on the piano.

The number "8" is based on the fact that the pipe sounding the bottom *c* on the manual 8′ open stop is about eight feet long. The pipe sounding tenor *c,* an octave higher on the same rank of pipes, is about one half as long, or four feet. Hence the following pitches in the table below are based on the same mathematical ratio and apply to manual stops. For exmple, the pipes of a 4′ stop are about half as long as those of an 8′ stop and sound an octave *higher*. A 16′ stop is

[5] In modern organs the viola usually has a foundational character like the violin diapason.

[6] Notable exception is the tremulant or tremolo, a special color device that you will not be needing for quite some time.

16

twice as long as an 8′ stop and sounds an octave *lower*. This formula is developed in the table below; see at the right the note which is heard when one plays a *c* while using the stops indicated to the left in the table.

16′	(sounds an octave below the note played)	*c*
8′	(normal pitch of the note played)	*c*
4′	(sounds an octave above the note played)	*c*
2 2/3′	(sounds twelfth above the note played)	*g*
2′	(fifteenth, two octaves above the note played)	*c*
1 3/5′	(seventeenth)	*e*
1 1/3′	(nineteenth)	*g*
1′	(twenty-second, three octaves above note played)	*c*

Stops sounding notes other than unison or octaves are called mutations, for example, the twelfth, seventeenth, and nineteenth in the table above.

ASSIGNMENT

Be prepared to tell the following at your next lesson:

1) Manual nomenclatures of your practice organs
2) The function of stop tablets and drawknobs
3) Significance of numbers on stop tablets
4) The two categories and four families of organ stops

17

2

PRACTICE PROCEDURES—
THE CRESCENDO—SWELL PEDALS

Practice Procedures

Under the guidance of your instructor you will now begin to practice, using simple combinations of stops. It is a good idea to use an individual stop for a complete study (particularly the basic ranks of 8′ pitch) in order to learn its *quality* and *volume*. Change to another stop and use it in the same manner. Selection of the most appropriate stops for a particular study or composition is a matter that requires much knowledge and experience. A few good combinations, however, are suggested for practice purposes. Select sparkling, light ones for music having rapid passages. For example:

1. flutes 8′ and 2′
2. bourdon 8′, octave 4′
3. stopped diapason 8′, nasard 2 2/3′
4. flute 8′, sifflöte 1′

For music of a quietly moving character such combinations as these might well suffice:

5. flutes 8′ and 4′
6. quintaton 8′, flute 4′

A selection of more robust character would sound well played on:

7. diapason 8′, octave 4′
8. diapason (principal) 8′, fifteenth (Great)
9. diapason 8′, principal 4′, plein jeu III (Swell)

In playing music of a quiet, sustained, or reflective character you might well use:

10. flute 8', viola 8'
11. gamba 8'

The Crescendo

Between the lowest manual and pedal board are located one, two, or more large pedals that affect the volume of tone. The one to the right is the crescendo pedal, a device that increases the volume of the organ ensemble by systematically adding stops, beginning with the soft stops and increasing to approximately full organ. This accessory has a limited use; in fact, you may not need it during your first year of study.

Swell Pedals

The expression or swell pedals to the left of the crescendo operate louvers that open or close to increase or decrease the volume of tone in particular divisions, each of which is enclosed in a separate swell chamber or swell box. Remember, we noted earlier that some divisions are completely unenclosed. The sections that are most commonly enclosed are the Swell, Choir, and Solo, though you may even find that the Great division on small organs has been enclosed to give added flexibility for performing certain music.

The absence of an expression pedal for an organ or division is an indication that the pipes of that division are exposed, though they may be behind a screen or curtain. In the early stages of study, as you begin to practice, be sure that all swell boxes are open. If a certain combination seems too loud for a piece you wish to play, it is better to secure a quieter, more suitable combination rather than to practice with the boxes closed. Not only does closing the boxes change the volume of tone of the stops inside the box but the harmonics are in part absorbed, resulting in *some* change of quality as well.

3

COUPLERS—ADDITIONAL PRACTICE PROCEDURES—OTHER MECHANICAL CONTROLS

Couplers

On consoles having stops arranged in rows—tilting tablets or other forms of "stop tablets"—you can see to the extreme right of any group, representing the voices of a division, one or more tablets that are called couplers. They are sometimes black and have white lettering to distinguish them from other controls. On a console with draw-knobs these couplers are located in two different places: (*a*) at the top of a group of manual draw-knobs and designed as draw-knobs themselves—*intramanual* couplers; and (*b*) in the center of the console above the top manual and designed as tilting tablets—*intermanual* couplers.

Intramanual couplers are used to alter the pitch of a given stop or stops within a division. For example, a Swell ensemble of diapason 8′ and principal 4′ with Swell to Swell 4′ coupler drawn gives basic pitches plus diapason 4′ and principal 2′. In other words, it *adds an octave above whatever stops are already drawn on the manual.*

Intermanual couplers are used to transfer stops from one manual to another. For example, stops drawn on the Swell may be transferred or added to a Great ensemble by drawing the Swell to Great 8′ coupler. To draw a Swell to Great 4′ coupler transfers to the Great pitches an octave above whatever stops are drawn on the Swell.

Additional Practice Procedures

As you continue your pedal practice you may wish to couple manual stops to pedal to secure light, bright combinations, especially in small instruments where few pedal registers are available.

When you practice trios it is desirable to secure contrasted combinations on pedal and manuals. Try to secure contrasts of color and pitch while maintaining similar levels of volume. For example, you might try using 16′ and 8′ registers in pedal, 8′ and 2′ on one manual, and 8′ and 4′ on the other.

In playing ensemble passages, two simple solutions are possible: (a) Use independent pedal stops that *blend* in color and balance in volume. (b) Use a balanced manual combination coupled at 8′ pitch to pedal, adding pedal register 16′ that will balance in volume.

You are now ready to combine stops from various manuals, thus becoming better acquainted with the mechanics of couplers and learning to hear new combinations. Try an ensemble like the following, drawing Swell to Great 8′ and Choir to Great 8′; play on the Great manual.

Sw.[1]: flute 8′, principal 4′
Gr. : gemshorn 8′
Ch. : nason 8′, nasard 2 2/3′

Your instructor will help you find combinations suitable for the organs on which you practice.

Other Mechanical Controls

The console accessories described in the following paragraphs will not be needed for some time. You may read about them to satisfy your curiosity, or refer to this information when your instructor indicates that it will be needed for performance of music you are to study.

Pistons are devices for making quick stop changes, and they are round buttons located immediately below or above manuals and sometimes just above the pedal board. The latter are known as "toe studs" and are for operation by the foot in cases where the hands are too busy to depress the manually operated pistons. The

[1] The main divisions of the organ are abbreviated in reduced text: Sw. Swell, Gr. Great, Ch. Choir, Pos. Positiv.

various types of pistons can generally be changed easily at the console (see Chap. 14).

Individual *manual pistons* are attached to the manual of the division they operate. These may or may not affect pedal stops.

General pistons are designed to change pedal stops, manual stops, and all couplers.

Pedal pistons are designed to change pedal stops only.

Most modern American organs are generously supplied with these devices that aid in efficient operation of the organ. You will find on some consoles that general pistons are available for both finger and toe operation, sometimes as duplicates.

Similar are the *reversibles* which operate as follows: the Great to Pedal Reversible is located to the left of center below the Great keys where it is easily operated by the left thumb. This control adds the Great to Pedal 8′ coupler or, if that coupler is already on, retires it. Reversibles may be found for other manuals and may be duplicated by pedal studs, often located to the right above the pedal board.

The *sforzando* is a control that adds full organ. It is most frequently operable by the right toe of the player and is marked "sfz." This control may be duplicated by a manual piston as well. On some modern instruments two or three such "sfz" pistons are supplied that lead in stages to full organ, the last bringing in all remaining reeds and 16′ stops as well.

Various forms of *cancel* buttons are provided. They are most commonly marked by a cipher "0." These, when attached to particular manuals, retire all stops and intra-manual couplers of that division. There is usually a *general cancel*, most often located to the extreme right below the bottom manual, which retires all stops and couplers of the organ. This general cancel will not affect the crescendo pedal or sforzando in most organs, though the Schantz Company has that accessory wired to cancel the sforzando as well. In the Austin organ console, division cancels appear as long wooden strips above the stops themselves; they retire whatever stops lie immediately below them. In other consoles the individual manual cancels appear immediately above a "stop jamb" or group of draw-

22

knobs for a given division and are operated by simply depressing a small bar with the fingers.

4

ENSEMBLE BUILDING I

You are now ready to begin simple ensemble building, one of the most fascinating aspects of organ registration. Great variety is at your disposal, even with an organ of moderate size, the only limitation upon the effectiveness of your results being the extent of your own knowledge and good taste.

> As in all branches of learning, good taste must here be developed on a firm foundation of logic and tradition.

Individual initiative must follow careful development of fundamental understanding and knowledge.

Ensemble Building on the Individual Manual

Your first problem will be to construct simple foundational ensembles, omitting diapasons and using only flutes, strings, and well-blending hybrids.[1] Omission of the diapason, the most important

---

[1] These are flues with special characteristics drawn from the different families of tone, e.g., flute and string. PLEASE NOTE: Any register of string nomenclature must be truly foundational to serve in any ensemble and should be reserved for special color purposes if it is not.

and virile member of the flues, means that you are limited to a *mezzo-forte* to *forte* volume. You can build such an ensemble on each individual manual. Assume that you wish a gradual buildup of tone. First draw your soft flute 8′, then add flute 4′. Next you can draw the flute 2 2/3′ and finally piccolo 2′. It may prove desirable to draw the 2′ before the 2 2/3′, if the intensity of the two stops is equal. Although the term "foundation tone" is most accurately applied to flues of 8′ and 4′ pitch, it is used here to indicate all stops of the flue category which have well-blending qualities that make them suitable for ensemble purposes. In the process of buildup that you have begun here other foundational flues such as gemshorn 8′ or viola 8′—when this stop is not too stringy in quality—may be used to preserve a balance of tone between basic 8′ pitch and the higher pitched voices.

ASSIGNMENT

Work out the process described above on each manual, noting the order in which you add these stops and bring your results to your lesson.

Ensemble Building Using Couplers

You are now ready to begin another procedure in ensemble building, this time using couplers. For example, on a three-manual organ you can draw Swell to Choir 8′, Swell to Great 8′, and Choir to Great 8′. Begin by adding stops as above. You will note that this coupler arrangement will give three levels of volume (in order of increase) on the Swell, Choir, and Great. This is a basic approach to organ registration, and it is important to understand it thoroughly.

If your instrument is deficient in "upper work" (high pitched stops), you will need to draw 4′ couplers as you continue building. It is important to choose carefully the point at which you wish to draw these couplers. Under average circumstances they should *not* be drawn.

ASSIGNMENT

Record your procedure and bring the information to your lesson.

5

THE HARMONIC SERIES—MUTATIONS—MIXTURES

The Harmonic Series

Musical tones produced on different instruments can sound the same pitch (having the same number of vibrations per second) and yet have distinct qualities. The size and shape of the instrument as well as the material used for its construction determine the quality. Musical instruments produce not a pure tone—that is, all fundamental pitch—but a composite of fundamental and overtones, the latter being relatively soft and blending into this composite sound. The selection and intensity of overtones determine instrumental quality. The same reasoning applies to individual ranks of organ pipes. Their special tonal characteristics derive from their relative size, the construction of the mouth (and cap in stopped pipes), and even the material used to make them. From this you can see that the harmonic series has played an important role in organ design. Below is a diagram showing the notes that comprise the series.

1. 8′   — fundamental
2. 4′   — octave
3. 2 2/3′ — twelfth
4. 2′   — fifteenth
5. 1 3/5′ — seventeenth (tièrce)
6. 1 1/3′ — nineteenth (larigot)

7. 1 1/7′ — twenty-first, flatted (septième)
8. 1′ — twenty-second (sifflöte)

An understanding of many musical principles is related to this series, and if you memorize it, beginning with the fundamental (1) and including the first three octaves (through 8), you will have a basis for understanding important factors in branches of music other than the organ. You will note that these first eight notes of the harmonic series include the components of a dominant-seventh chord. Those tones shown in black in the diagram have an approximate intonation.

Early organ builders made use of various harmonics, including the twelfth, fifteenth, and seventeenth, to reinforce fundamentals, that is, stops of 8′ pitch. Mutations and mixtures resulted from these building practices.

Mutations

Generally of flute or diapason tone, mutations are essential to the buildup of tonal masses in organ registration.[1] They also aid in creating special color effects. Artful combining of flute mutations with stops of 8′ pitch can create voices of subtle and beautiful character. Properly balanced principal mutations reinforce the natural harmonics of a fundamental.[2] For example, the tonal buildup of a Great division is as follows:

(gemshorn 16′ or principal or violone)
diapason 8′ (principal)
octave 4′
twelfth 2 2/3′
fifteenth 2′

Due to its "scaling," or relatively small size, the twelfth will add vivacity and fire to chordal combinations to which it is added.

---

[1] Mutations are also developed from gemshorn, dulciana, and quintade pipes.
[2] You can usually determine the quality of a given mutation by its terminology. Those whose names are "spelled out" (e.g. twelfth, fifteenth) are generally principals. The flute mutations often have special names such as nasard and larigot.

26

Reference to the following table will give you a clear picture of the different series with octaves and mutations.

Fundamental 32′	16′	8′		4′
16′	8′	4′	(octave)	2′
10 2/3′	5 1/3′	2 2/3′	(nasard, nasat)	1 1/3′
8′	4′	2′	(fifteenth, piccolo)	1′
(6 2/5′)	(3 1/5′)	1 3/5′	(seventeenth, tièrce, terz)	
5 1/3′	2 2/3′	1 1/3′	(nineteenth, larigot)	
(4 4/7′)	(2 2/7′)	1 1/7′	(flatted twenty-first, septième)	
4′	2′	1′	(sifflöte)	

Although it would be a waste of time to memorize this entire table, it can serve you well for convenient reference. You should study the 8′ series as a basis for manual tonal buildup. Similarly the 16′ series can be used as a basis for pedal buildup; beginning an octave lower than the 8′ series, the "number names" of its components are achieved by simply multiplying by two those of the 8′ series.

Mixtures

Mixtures are compound stops used either for solo or ensemble purposes, depending upon their design. Drawing a single stop knob will bring on the two or more ranks of pipes of a mixture. A *grave mixture* on the Great of a small organ may simply be a combination of twelfth and fifteenth to be drawn above a diapason 8′ and octave 4′ to complete a Great ensemble. Large organs with flue ensembles like that mentioned above, reaching from the 16′ pitch to the 2′ pitch, generally contain also one or more compound stops or mixtures that carry the pitch and brilliance of the division higher than otherwise possible.

A feature of *ensemble mixtures* is their construction which "breaks" in its ascent. The diagram following represents a characteristic three-rank mixture with breaks. It shows how the highest pitched rank drops back or breaks at certain points—varied by each

27

builder to his special "recipes"—and explains, too, how brilliance is added to the low register and gravity to the high register. You can readily see that such a mixture in its lowest octave adds relatively *acute* pitches (fifteenth, nineteenth, and twenty-second). In the high register, however, due to breaking, its pitches are all relatively *grave* (octave, twelfth, and fifteenth).

The cymbal (an acute mixture) sometimes breaks in every octave and repeats.

You can see why breaks should not occur in a mixture intended for *solo* use, as any leaps down would be obvious here, though they go unnoticed in a complex of chordal tones.

Mixtures intended primarily for *ensemble* use contain generally only octave- and fifth-sounding ranks. Adding the third (seventeenth) can create clashing effects.[3] For example, holding a C major chord on a stop of 8′ pitch and adding the twelfth adds to that chord *b* and *d*, but adding a tièrce brings a *g*-sharp into the combination as well (actually it adds the three tones *e*, *g*-sharp, and *b*).

Harmonics is a compound stop including tièrce and septième ranks which through careful voicing has been made usable in chordal combinations. It is not commonly employed, however, in a principal buildup or in full organ but for special color.

Some ensemble mixtures are:

Acuta: (L. *acutus*=sharp) G. akuta, scharf; D. scherp; G. zimbel or cymbel; F. cymbale. These are high-pitched mixtures.

Mixtur(e): G. F. fourniture, plein-jeu, S. lleno, I. ripieno. These are basic mixtures of two or more ranks.

[3] Occasionally third-sounding ranks can be employed in very acute mixtures, especially those designed to be used with reeds.

Some solo mixtures are:

Sesquialtera: Named for the interval of a sixth formed by its 2 2/3' and 1 3/5' ranks (sounding *g* and *e* above a *c*). Exceptionally it can be a three- or four-rank mixture. This stop is combined with an 8' stop for solo purposes.

Tertian: Sounds the interval of a third. In 8' series it contains 1 3/5' and 1 1/3' (*e* and *g* above a *c*).

Carillon: Though a name usually given tubular bells, this terminology is also applied to a three-rank mixture with prominent third-sounding rank.

Cornet: A favored flute mixture. In a five-rank cornet the following pitches are usually present: 8', 4', 2 2/3', 2' and 1 3/5'. Note the tièrce on top of the series.

ASSIGNMENT

1) Define a mutation.

2) Tell two ways in which mutations are employed.

3) Define a mixture.

4) What is meant by "breaking" in a mixture? What useful purpose does this constructive principle serve?

5) What is the prime difference between esemble and solo mixtures?

6) Name some ensemble mixtures. Name some solo mixtures.

7) What do the terms *acute* and *grave* mean as applied to mixtures?

6

REEDS AND HYBRID STOPS

Reeds

As we mentioned in Chap. 1, the reeds fall into two classes, generally speaking. Their tone is produced by a metal tongue that vibrates against a shallot or reed in the base of the pipe. We find open and stopped pipes of various shapes and varying reed treatment, which develops special characteristics.

Chorus reeds form the equivalent of the brass of an orchestra, adding power and richness. They vary in tonal color from the relatively smooth, broad tuba tone to the brilliant, edgy tone of the bombarde, a French type reed. Typical examples are: bassoon (I. fagotto), bombarde, clarion (F. clairon), cornopean, flügelhorn, oboe (F. hautbois, meaning "high woodwind"), oboe clarion, ophicleide (named from an ancestor of the tuba), trombone (G. posaune), trumpet (I. tromba), trompette. These reeds can also serve as solo voices.

Solo, or orchestral, *reeds* are imitative in quality. They are generally omitted in ensembles due to their poor blending qualities. Typical examples are: clarinet, cor anglais (English horn), corno d' amore, corno di bassetto, French horn, orchestral oboe.

Some reeds of early origin which prove useful for solo and ensemble purposes are: cromorne (G. krummhorn, also spelled cormorne), dulcian, regal, singend regal (a high pitched pedal reed).

Hybrid Stops

We find stops which borrow characteristics from more than one family. These are called *hybrid stops*. Such is the flexible gemshorn, a tapered stop whose sound is somewhere between that of flute and string. The excellent blending quality of this stop makes it useful for manual 16′ stops as well as mutations. It is closely related to the spitzflöte which differs in having a higher cut mouth, giving a somewhat less stringy quality, and a more moderate taper.

ASSIGNMENT

1) For trio playing you now can vary your schemes for combining stops. Experiment with varying registers and families, aiming at balance in volume but contrast in character. It is feasible, for example, to combine salicional 8′ and nasard 2 2/3′ to form a "synthetic oboe" on one part, against diapason 8′ in the second manual and bourdon 16′ and flute 8′ in the pedal. You can use flute 8′, nasard and piccolo 2′ with tièrce 1 3/5′ to form a *cornet*, especially useful in playing solo lines in early music.

2) Make as many trio combinations as you can, taking full advantage of the varied color to be had from use of mutations, noting these examples on paper and bringing them to your lesson.

3) Listen to the recording "The King of Instruments," Vol. I.[1] This is a delightful lecture by the late G. Donald Harrison, former president of the Aeolian-Skinner Company, describing the different families of tone color. Make a note of any questions you may have concerning the lecture demonstration and bring them to your lesson.

[1] Aeolian-Skinner Organ Co., Boston 25, Mass.

7
ECHO STOPS–CÉLESTES– THE TREMULANT

There are three types of stops we have not discussed, and these form a part of the special color effects of the organ.

Echo Stops

Echo stops, constructed in relatively small sizes, are miniatures of various flues; their soft and gentle quality makes them particularly appealing for service playing or for music of romantic character. Some examples are:

diapason echo stops (dulciana, dolce, dolcan, dulcet)
flute echo stops (flauto amabile, flauto dolce, flûte d'amour)
string echo stops (echo viole, echo gamba, aeoline, viole sourdine)

Céleste

Célestes are created by combining a regular tuned rank with a sharp tuned or flat tuned rank of equivalent quality and dynamic level to give an undulating effect, for example, gamba céleste, voix céleste (vox céleste), unda maris, erzähler céleste, flute céleste, gemshorn céleste. A single stop knob may draw two ranks to form a céleste, or one rank (the sharp tuned one) must be combined with the adjacent knob operating the regular tuned rank. The latter arrangement has the advantage of allowing the use of the very soft rank without Céleste effect; for example, dulciana and unda maris are separate ranks which when combined form a céleste, but the dulciana can also be used alone. There is a mistaken notion among some organists that célestes are a new addition to the large family of organ stops, but this is not true. The early Italian organ boasted a mistuned rank that was combined with the principale 8' to form a céleste, and the unda maris was already in use in Bach's time.

The Tremulant

The tremulant (or tremolo) is considered a stop, although it is not a rank of pipes but rather a mechanical device that creates a regular pulsation in the wind pressure supplied to chests, producing an unusual and interesting effect. The tremulant, too, is a time honored device, though some organists are known to avoid it like the plague. Indeed, nothing can sound quite so bad as an ill adjusted or too violent tremulant, and the effectiveness of the device is to be considered in inverse proportion to the extent of its use. It serves best on light, delicate combinations—solo or ensemble—especially where there is a relatively static series of chords in the texture of the music being performed. Needless to say, its use in loud combinations is something to be avoided.

8

ENSEMBLE BUILDING II

It is obvious that you can build a good flue ensemble (granted you have a large enough instrument) with diapason and upper work, or you can build with *all* flues. Greater clarity can be achieved by omission of duplications that occur when softer flues are added to diapason work. If a gradual buildup in tone is desired, the use of flutes and other soft flues can facilitate the process. The resulting ensemble will have a thicker or more opaque quality that can be useful in music of romantic character. As we shall note later, performance of certain music, particularly very early music, requires that stops of the flute and diapason families *not* be mixed.

Care should be taken in ensemble building to avoid the following: (*a*) any célestes, (*b*) stops of thick quality which would obscure the movement of voices of a contrapuntal texture (tibia or too broadly voiced diapasons), (*c*) any penetrating and ill-blending stops (piercing, large scaled gambas), (*d*) or any stops intended for pure solo or orchestral effects (vox humana with the "nailed down" tremolo). Echo stops are relatively useless in ordinary ensembles. Their omission is consistent with a policy that might be called "economy of registration": a good artistic approach and one that will serve to give greater efficiency later on when you use the combination action of a large instrument.

ASSIGNMENT

1) With ample diapasons available, form choruses on separate manuals.

2) Using unison couplers to the Great manual, form a diapason ensemble. Proper voicing of stops of the Swell organ generally assures one successful use of the Swell to Great 4′ coupler—in case sufficient upper work is lacking. If no mixtures are available on the Great, the Great to Great 4′ coupler can probably be used to "top off" the ensemble.

With ample mixtures available on the Great, it is not good to add the 4′ intramanual coupler; in fact, a terrible, shrieking quality is likely to result if super couplers are employed with acute mixtures! [1] A good rule is to avoid use of a 4′ coupler on any ensemble that employs stops of higher than 2′ pitch.

If your organ is deficient in diapason upper work, you must obtain needed richness, for example on the Swell, by drawing bright flute registers with the diapason 8′ and employing the super coupler. Such an approach should be employed only as a matter of expediency.

3) Use the entire flue work to build an ensemble, beginning with flutes and strings 8′ such as viola but not viole or salicional, flutes 4′, hybrids 8′ and 4′, mild diapasons, flutes 2 2/3′ and 2′ such as nasard and piccolo or octavin from Swell and/or Choir, strong secondary diapa-

---

[1] The term "super" applies to the 4′ couplers and "sub" to 16′ couplers.

sons and octaves, and, finally, Great diapason 8′, Swell and/or Choir mixtures, the remainder of the Great diapason chorus, and the Great mixtures. The exact sequence will vary with the instrument, but the plan given here can serve as a guide. This type of ensemble serves best in music of a romantic character; you may, therefore, wish to reserve study of this ensemble plan until such time as you have specific use for it.

Since no single feature of organ registration is of greater importance than the thorough understanding and efficient application of ensemble building techniques, you should study each organ at your disposal and practice this buildup. Make notes of your results for discussion at your lesson. One further possibility not mentioned is starting with soft flues and later retiring these as diapason tone is introduced, in this manner always maintaining maximum clarity.

The Pedal Organ

The division most likely to be deficient in American organs is that supplied for the pedal organ. Basic approaches for increase of tone learned in dealing with manual problems can, at least to some extent, be applied here. You will by this time be able to judge a good tonal balance. In polyphonic music it is advantageous to maintain balance between the pedal and manual work, while at the same time keeping the Pedal somewhat contrasted in quality. If ample stops are available, the problem is not great; however, if only a few 16′ stops are at hand and few or no 8′ stops (perish the thought!), you must rely on the use of couplers to secure proper balance at the expense of the desirable independence to be gained from use of separate registers in the Pedal.

It is sometimes feasible to secure balance and contrast on secondary manuals thus: Play a choir ensemble and rely on Swell to Pedal coupler for pedal tone. If, on the other hand, considerable tone is required and coupling is indicated to secure this required level of tone, you must couple to Pedal whatever manuals are in use. For example, if you combine Swell and Choir, you couple these manuals to Pedal. When Swell, Choir, and Great are employed, they are likewise coupled to Pedal, and when super couplers are added to the manual ensemble, balance can be secured by drawing super

35

couplers to Pedal (if, indeed, there are any to draw!). Much experimentation is necessary to get the best results in use of the Pedal organ.

16' Manual Tone

Little has been said of the use of 16' tone in manual work. Unless reasonably clear tone is available, the 16' manual stops are best avoided. The 16' bourdon (or lieblichgedeckt) so often found on Swell organs is poor in ensembles. The gemshorn and quintatön, as well as the violone for heavier than average ensembles are generally satisfactory. Note that these are flues with considerable harmonic development and relatively weak foundational pitch. These useful flues of 16' pitch can be added to very clear ensembles without excessive thickness; in fact, the gravity thus attained is often essential to balance of upper work for climactic situations. It is worthy of note that 16' manual registers seldom figure in polyphonic music, except for such climaxes. Special cases involving use of tone of 16' pitch in manual work will be discussed later.

9

USE OF THE REEDS

The reed stops offer great color variety in organ registration. (a) They are excellent sources of solo tone, whether soft (corno d'amore) or loud (trumpet). (b) They give power and weight (trumpet) as well as brilliance (bombarde, clarion) to an ensemble. (*c*) They serve ably in lending special color for romantic music. For example, the clarinet, a solo reed, can give an eerie, foreboding sound when used for low-pitched, soft chords. The French horn is useful, too, in short chord successions, and indeed, you can employ almost any solo-type reed for special effect in a homophonic passage. It is well to remember that the effectiveness of such means is in inverse proportion to the length of their use.

A solo reed can be subtly changed through addition of mutation (s) . Use of flute 4′ or nasard 2 2/3′, for example, with solo reed of 8′ pitch is feasible. Combining 8′ flue tone with 8′ reed solos is of questionable value, and it should be done only where extra weight is desired or where a thick tone is required. In other words, *as a rule, we "alter"* a solo reed to best advantage by adding pitches other than that of the reed itself.

The best use of reeds in building ensemble, particularly in romantic music, is simply to combine them in the course of buildup of the flues, as described in Chap. 8, bringing them in as their pitch and volume would dictate. For example, softer 8′ reeds may be added after light diapasons, the heavier reeds like the trumpet being brought in last. The quality chosen for 16′ manual reeds is such that they can usually be safely employed without great loss of clarity. The bassoon is a favorite stop for this, as is the bombarde, where brilliance and fire are needed with large flue ensembles. The reeds are fused with the flue chorus through employment of mixtures.

You can often make use of a simple reed chorus; for example, bassoon 16′, trumpet 8′, and clarion 4′. Reeds can be combined with mixtures for a fiery sound.

We note in passing that the flue work is basic to performing the organ music of Bach that falls into ensemble categories. Good use however, can be made in building ensembles, especially on small instruments, through judicious addition of reeds; one had better omit those which are too heavy or broad to "speak" promptly. Use of 16′ or 8′ reed in pedals is common in baroque music for emphasizing climactic entries of thematic material, though care must be taken never to play such combinations faster than the pipes can speak properly. The nature of the reeds available and the tempo of the music will have to determine whether or not their use is advantageous. For further discussion of this point see the chapter on registration of the music of Bach (pages 114-15).

ASSIGNMENT

1) Practice building ensemble with flues and reeds. Be prepared to demonstrate this at your lesson.

2) Prepare to demonstrate several combinations of *various* pitches employing (*a*) reeds and mixtures, (*b*) reeds and mutations, and (*c*) reeds and diapasons.

Ger. Prinzipal Fr. Montre
Diapason = foundation tone of the organ
When at its best, it is singularly pure and simple
Almost entirely free from harmonic overtones or upper
partials. It is its simple quality which makes the
Diapason tone the proper foundation of the tonal
structure of the organ.

10

UNIFICATION AND DUPLEXING

Two features of organ design that have been used extensively in constructing small practice organs are unification and duplexing. By this time you may have discovered some of the basic principles employed through experimentation.

Unification

Simply stated, unification is the use of more than one pitch from a single rank of pipes. It is not uncommon to find on small instruments the use of several pitches from a given rank. For instance, on the Swell organ the flute 8' is frequently used at 4' pitch and sometimes at 16', 2 2/3', and 2' pitches as well. Certainly unification is defensible, especially where it is used with discretion, in that it provides a flexibility not otherwise available in a low-priced installation or one where limitations of space would forbid having such extra pitches if additional ranks were required for each. The disadvantage of this system becomes obvious when we reflect that part of the special character of organ tone results from *varied color* of its component members, as well as subtle differences in intensity. When we use four pitches from a single stopped flute, we have gained flexibility at the expense of richness in their combination. Also it is obvious that, if we draw a flute 8′ and flute 4′ and add to this the Swell super coupler, we add two stops, a flute 4′ and 2′—*if* both stops are independent. If these stops are members of the same rank, our super coupler will bring on *only* a flute 2′, as the flute 4′ is already present. Such duplications, multiplied by the number of unifications, can be weakening in ensemble work.

Limited unification is, however, commonly employed by good builders who frequently use a second pitch or more rarely three from a single rank.

Duplexing

Duplexing is the term often applied to the use of an organ stop on more than one manual. The most common use occurs in small practice organs where space and economy demand the greatest flexibility of design. For example, a flute 8′ may, through proper wiring, be played from both Swell and Great manuals; a viola 8′ may likewise be duplexed. The obvious advantage here is that you can accompany a viola solo on the flute, whereas if these stops were present only on one of the two manuals, this flexibility would be lost. Here again we find a regrettable feature accompanies a good one. Coupling the Swell to the Great will reinforce your Great ensemble in those registers *only* where duplexing is not involved.

It would seem that coupling in instruments such as that mentioned here would be pointless. In actual practice, builders often have the good judgment to combine unification with duplexing, giving to Swell and Great organs at least *some* contrasting members, so that coupling can be used to advantage. For example, an organ with four ranks of pipes—diapason, flute, dulciana, and salicional—

may have as its Swell specification: bourdon 16′, stopped flute 8′, salicional 8′, flute 4′, salicet 4′ nasard 2 2/3′, orchestral oboe 8′—a synthetic stop formed by combining salicional 8′ with nasard 2 2/3′—and piccolo 2′; while the Great specification might be: diapason 8′, melodia 8′—the same flute as that used on the Swell, but with an inaccurate name—dulciana 8′, octave 4′, flute 4′ and dulcet 4′. In this case, to couple the Swell to the Great would add stops not already sounding on the Great, namely bourdon 16′, salicional 8′, nasard 2 2/3′, salicet 4′, and piccolo 2′—assuming full organ is to be used. On an *independent* organ, one where duplexing is totally absent, we would have *also* the addition to Great of the following from Swell: stopped flute 8′, flute 4′. Thus we see an obviously weak feature of duplexing.

Fortunately the procedures just mentioned are being eliminated in practice organs being built today. Most builders employ both unification and duplexing in small installations but avoid duplication of both pitch and quality on the two manuals. For instance, if a quintaton 8′ on the Great is duplexed for use at 16′ pitch in the Pedal, no defect results in the ensemble. A principal 4′ may be used on Great and the same rank of pipes duplexed for Positiv principal 2′. Or a flute 8′ with unified 4′ on Positiv may be used for Pedal bourdon 16′. Such installations as the one described here are developed along traditional lines of organ building and all pipes are likely to be unenclosed, whereas an organ designed on the dated principles previously described will likely be entirely enclosed in a single swell box.

ASSIGNMENT

1) Analyze each practice organ you use to determine the extent to which unification and duplexing have been employed and report your findings at your lesson. To check unification on a manual flute, draw the 8′ stop and play a chord. Then retire the 8′ and draw the 4′, playing the same chord an octave lower. If the sound is *identical,* unification is employed. Checking duplexing involves the comparing of registers in different divisions. You may even find that a builder has allowed his imagination to take wings and given a single rank of pipes different names on two different manuals.

2) See if you can locate any unification or duplexing in the large instrument (s) at your disposal. Watch especially for "borrowed" (duplexed) pedal stops and for unification within the Swell and Choir organs.

11

DIVISION ANALYSIS

At this stage it is clear that your success in effective ensemble building rests largely on your knowledge of your instrument. Unless you have a clear conception of what each division of the organ contains by way of resources, you may be unduly slow in securing desired effects and thereby waste valuable time. The problem is twofold: You must first analyze what a piece requires in tonal resources, and then secure it promptly. With this thought in mind it will be advantageous to review the various divisions and recapitulate what you can *expect* to find.[1]

The Great

You have already learned the components of the Great diapason chorus. Ideally diapason ranks of 16', 8', 2 2/3', and 2' are included.

---

[1] Though it is quite true that there is a great variation in the resources of organs and in the components of individual divisions, the generalizations given here are based on an accepted norm. The object of learning the material, then, is to give the student a knowledge of what divisions often contain and, more important, to teach the value of rapid division analysis as a means of effective handling of any instrument, no matter how it may differ from the norm furnished by most organs.

(The 16′ may be a violone, gemshorn, or quintaton.) These are crowned by a fourniture IV and possibly a scharf III.

If you are limited to a small chorus it may contain principal 8′, octave 4′, (twelfth), and fifteenth. This then is the most important and basic part of your Great. You are likely to have soft stops as well. Soft flues may include bourdon 8′, gemshorn 8′, flute 4′. There may be also a large reed such as bombarde or trumpet to use with massave effects or for solo purposes. The basic part of the Great is still its diapason chorus, and for ordinary ensemble purposes it is very easy to build from bottom to top. Sometimes you may wish to add the 2′ rank before the twelfth in order to keep an octave- rather than a fifth-sounding rank at the top of your tonal mass. This is by no means obligatory if voicing and blend of the chorus components are good.

The Swell

The dominant color of the full Swell organ is a blaze of glory formed by a reed chorus and mixture.[2] This can be demonstrated simply. First, draw all ensemble flues. Play a chord. Then add reed chorus and mixture and play the same chord again. Following that retire all stops except the reed chorus and mixture and repeat the chord. You will note that taking away the soft flues has little effect on the volume and brilliance of your ensemble; opacity in the foundational registers disappears. This proves the statement previously made that reeds and mixture dominate the Swell ensemble!

The Swell offers more variety than the Great, and generally has more stops. First, we find a complement of diapason stops such as geigen principal 8′, principal 4′, plein jeu III. In cases where an 8′ principal is missing, it is usually supplied by a foundational flute and/or string. If the flute is sufficiently broad in character, it alone may serve in the 8′ register. Besides the diapasons you can usually

---

[2] Although the Swell organ of small instruments may be lacking in a reed chorus or mixture, these are the resources normally desired. A great literature has been developed in which such resources are desirable; the tradition is particularly important as it relates to proper performance of French, English, and American organ music of particular periods.

expect to find the following flutes: lieblichgedeckt 16′, rohrflöte 8′, harmonic flute 4′, (nasard 2 2/3′), piccolo 2′. You can also expect to find a reed chorus: fagotto 16′, trumpet 8′, and clarion 4′. Special effect stops may include a string and céleste—viola and viola céleste or gambe and voix céleste—and soft reeds such as the vox humana.

In summing up the resources of the Swell you see that you can build (*a*) an ensemble of soft flues, (*b*) an ensemble of diapason tone, (*c*) an ensemble of only reeds, (*d*) an ensemble of reed and mixture, or (*e*) a weighty ensemble containing flutes, well-blending strings, reeds, and mixtures. It only remains to know which of these varied effects is required by the music to be played to pull out quickly the stops you wish.

The Choir

The Choir division will vary with the size of an organ. It may be a substitute for the Positiv of the baroque period (G. Rückpositiv, so named as it is an unenclosed division located *behind* [*zurück*] the organist in the organ loft). In many organs of past years the Choir contained largely flue work suitable for accompaniment playing. On a large instrument there may be stops allowing use of the division for either of these purposes, that is, for accompanimental work or for proper performance of baroque literature. There is generally at least one solo reed here, perhaps a céleste also.

On an ample Choir organ you are likely to find a good complement of flutes, some of which may have "classic voicing," which though good in itself can create problems in the performance of some romantic literature, particularly French music from about the middle of the nineteenth century until the present time.[3] Flutes

---

[3] Although it is beyond the scope of the present work to deal in any detail with specific characteristics of construction that create voicing, and the student will need to rely on the experience and mature judgment of his instructor in learning what constitutes classic and romantic tone in organ stops, a few generalizations may prove helpful.

Certain voices may be classified on the basis of the period of their introduction to the organ; e.g., the clarinet is a *relatively* late stop. Romantic voicing tends to give breadth of tone with emphasis on the basic pitch of a stop rather than on its harmonic qualities. These stops, sometimes created for solo purposes, can prove poor in blending with other stops; examples are the tibia and many times the tuba

may include nason 8′, koppelflöte 4′, nasard 2 2/3′, and blockflöte 2′, (tièrce 1 3/5′). The dulciana and unda maris 8′ are common in the Choir, as is the clarinet. If the division doubles as Positiv, the solo reed may be one of baroque character such as the krummhorn 8′.

Solo and Positiv

The fourth manual is generally a Solo or Positiv. If a Solo division, it will include large-scaled flues—generally several of 8′ pitch, big reeds on somewhat heavier than ordinary pressure, and possibly imitative reeds such as English horn, orchestral oboe.

The Positiv will include a buildup of tone from basic pitch to very high ones. Despite relatively small scaling of its stops, this division makes a fine foil to the Great in early music due to its clearness and the advantage of its unenclosed placement. Characteristic might be an ensemble including the following: nasonflöte 8′, nachthorn 4′, nasard 2 2/3′, principal 2′, larigot 1 1/3′, sifflöte 1′, zimbel III. A baroque reed (such as rohrschalmei 8′) or even a reed chorus—dulcian 16′, krummhorn 8′, rohrschalmei 4′—might be found.

Obviously the simplicity and ordering of stops on the Positiv does not leave much choice in arrangement of stops, if you wish to build from soft to loud. There are no "alternate" stops in a given pitch (except for reeds). For color effects, you can choose a few pitches, for example: nasonflöte 8′ and nachthorn 4′; nasonflöte 8′ and principal 2′; or nasonflöte 8′, nachthorn 4′, and larigot 1 1/3′. Almost any combination of stops is satisfactory as long as it suits the character of the music being played. One useful device is to secure variety by playing stops in other than their normal pitch. For instance, if you are not satisfied with the sound of the nasonflöte 8′ and nachthorn 4′ in a given passage, try the nachthorn 4′ and princi-

---

mirabilis. A higher than normal wind pressure is sometimes required for these stops. They utilize excessive nicking at the windway to facilitate prompt speech.

Classic stops are, on the other hand, voiced to speak on low-wind pressures and blend in ensemble. They are seldom of excessive volume of tone, and they speak with clarity. These stops, generally having little or no nicking, may speak with a "chiff"; that is, they may produce a transient wind sound before their tone is heard.

pal 2′, playing your passage an octave *lower* than written. This process can be effective in the use of individual stops as well.

The Pedal

Similarly the Pedal organ will contain principal, flute, possibly string, and hybrid tone. If there is a good violone 16′, it may often be used as a basis for building where a principal 16′ is too weighty for a given manual ensemble for which it supplies a bass. You are fortunate if you have also flutes as well as bourdons, and still more fortunate if you have a few good borrowed stops like the quintaton, gemshorn, rohrgedeckt in 16′ and 8′ pitches, allowing for drawing these registers in various combinations without use of couplers.

Reviewing the material covered thus far, you see the following manuals used for particular purposes, and containing particular resources:

Gr.: diapason chorus (soft flutes, reed)
Sw.: full flues dominated by reed and mixture tone (a few effect stops such as célestes and reeds of solo or special-color value)
Ch.: flutes and mutation (s) (solo reed) *(for acc. playing)*
Solo: weighty flues and heavy reeds
Pos.: bright ensemble voices (solo reed)

Once you know these basic components, you can analyze the music to be played and decide upon registration needed for proper interpretation as to period and style (in the absence of definite instructions), and then pull out the stops.

ASSIGNMENT

1) Be able to tell at your next lesson the basic components of the average division: Great, Swell, Choir, Positiv, Solo, Pedal.

2) Determine where the following would be played:

(*a*) A cornet made up of flute and mutations and octaves

(*b*) Romantic music requiring massive dynamic gradation without change of stops

(*c*) Bold diapason chorus

(d) Bright diapason chorus, not too heavy

(e) Brilliant flue work without too much weight

(f) Light weight solo reeds

(g) Rich, heavy reeds

(h) Célestes

(i) Soft accompanimental voices, beginning with most likely stops and including other possibilities. State when you might use one or the other.

(j) Romantic string combination *piano, mezzo-piano*

12

MANUAL NOMENCLATURES

Certain difficulties arise in the interpretation of manual indications that should be clarified at an early stage in the study of organ music. American and English editions generally indicate a system of numbering from the bottom manual upward that leads to confusion. Reference to page 14 will show that on a two-manual organ the Great is Manual I and the Swell is Manual II. On a three-manual instrument, however, the Choir becomes Manual I; the Great, Manual II; and the Swell, Manual III. It is clear, then, that in making use of registration indications the performer must first know for *what kind of instrument* the indications are given.

The French and German approach is logical. Here the Great is always Manual I, and the Choir (Positiv or Rückpositiv) is Manual II. Any other manuals are numbered in the usual manner, from the

The American-Scandinavian Foundation
15 East 65ᵗʰ Street
New York, NY 10021

Studying Abroad Begins Right at Home…

bottom upward. One good reason for this system is that on French and German instruments the location of Great and Positiv may be interchanged, and the use of the Manual I indication for Great, regardless of its location, avoids a good deal of confusion. In the traditional organ, also, these two manuals, that is, the Great and its foil, the Positiv or Choir, are the most important. Since its invention in England in 1712 by Jordan, the swell box (enclosing ranks of the Swell organ) has gained in favor, particularly in England, France, and later in America. The accessory is still not considered of great enough value in Germany to be represented on all instruments being designed today. For instance, a large four-manual instrument may have *one* swell division (that is, enclosed division) or it may have *none*. In the summer of 1960 the writer had planned programs of American and German contemporary music for performance in Germany on two large four-manual instruments, both rebuilt within the previous decade. For the organ in the Hauptkirche St. Petri in Hamburg the program included a highly romantic piece, "Arioso" by Leo Sowerby, requiring considerable use of expression pedals. Lo and behold, the crescendo pedal (rollschweller) and expressive division (Schwellwerk) had both been removed from the organ as "unsatisfactory accessories"! Needless to say, the music had a lovely and elegant sound without the use of a single expressive division. A little opening and closing of the cupboard-like doors of the Brustwerk at a couple of points gave a slightly more romantic effect than might have resulted otherwise.

In addition to the manuals studied in Chap. 11, American organs often have a Bombarde organ, including brilliant French reeds and mixtures. With a growing conviction that the traditional organ is the true organ, the inclusion of floating string divisions has waned if not completely disappeared. Much more useful is an Antiphonal organ, a division which can aid in supporting congregational singing in large buildings. It is generally placed in the rear of the building in the place once occupied by a relatively useless Echo division that had only a few ethereal voices usable on rare occasions. One of the greatest installations of recent times in America is that built by the Aeolian-Skinner Organ Company of Boston for the Conference Chamber of the Auditorium in Independence, Missouri, headquarters of the Reorganized Church of Jesus Christ of Latter Day Saints. The organ of the auditorium (seating 5,754 persons) has 101 ranks and 5,591 pipes. Its Antiphonal organ is playable from the main console as well as from its own two-manual console located in the rear choir loft. Specifications for the Antiphonal organ are as follows:

Great (open chest)	*Pedal*
8′ Bourdon	16′ Bourdon
8′ Spitzflöte	8′ Principal
4′ Principal	
Mixtur (IV Ranks)	

Swell (enclosed)
8′ Viola
8′ Rohrflöte
4′ Gemshorn
8′ Trompette   Couplers (Swell 4′, Swell 16′)

Obviously such an organ is a respectable instrument within itself.

The Bombarde organ (open chest) on the same instrument is a fine example of such a division:

16′ Bombarde
 8′ Trompette Harmonique
 4′ Clairon Harmonique
    Tièrce Mixture (V-IX Ranks)
 8′ Trompette-en-Chamade

Of special interest are the Tièrce Mixture and the Trompette-en-Chamade. The latter is simply a horizontal trumpet stop sending its tone in the most direct fashion into the body of the building rather than by reflecting from a ceiling. The inclusion of a tièrce rank in the mixture makes this stop particularly suitable with French bombardes, a frequent requirement in the literature of that country. More will be said of this in the chapter on French organs.

Manuals are named in the instruments of foreign countries from their location, function, or some peculiarity of their components. In the German organ the following are characteristic:

Hauptwerk: main division (literally, "head work").
Rückpositiv: unenclosed division behind the organist.
Brustwerk: "breast work," located above console in a cupboard-like box with closing doors.
Brustpositiv: unenclosed division above console.
Oberwerk: brilliant division placed high in the organ case; this division is considered the main division where no Hauptwerk is indicated.
Unterwerk: "under work," a division placed low in the case.
Seitenwerk: side organ (s).
Schwellwerk: "swell work," enclosed or expressive division.
Kronwerk: "crown work," an organ crowning the various other divisions.
Hornwerk: Horn organ, a romantic development similar to Solo.
Echo: enclosed division, a romantic development.
Pedal: Pedal organ.

In French organs the following nomenclatures are found:

Grand Orgue: Great.
Positif: unenclosed (and later, sometimes enclosed!) Choir.
Bombarde: bright reed (s).
Récit: enclosed division, Swell organ.
Echo: division in a box to give faraway effect.
Solo: usually enclosed Solo organ.
Pedale: Pedal organ.

In Spanish organs the following are encountered:

Cadireta: first manual, Choir (Teclado Secundario or secondary division).
Organo Grande: Great organ, main manual (Teclado Principal).
Eco: Echo.
Recitatif: enclosed division containing voices suitable for melodic passages, possibly with céleste and voix humaine.
Pedaleira Agudos: the Pedal, generally very limited.

In the Italian organ, as in the German, manuals are often only denoted by number, and for many years the organs of Italy were limited to a single manual.

49

Organo di risposta: a relatively small division, lower manual.
Organo Grande: second manual, Great.

In relatively late Italian instruments are to be found enclosed Choir and Positiv and Swell. Germani gives details of an organ built about 1780 for St. Peter's Church, Trapani, which had seven manuals and pedals.[1] Three manuals were placed as usual, and two more on each side. Another oddity of some Italian organs was a coupler enabling the organist to play pedal registers on the manual, doubtless a handy device.

In the Dutch organ nomenclatures are as follows:

Groot Manuaal: Great.
Bovenwerk: "above" work, Oberwerk.
Rugpositief: rear unenclosed division, Rückpositiv.
Pedaal: Pedal organ.
Onderwerk: division placed in a low position, Unterwerk.
Brost-Clavier: "breast manual," placed centrally above keyboards.
Hoofd Manuaal: "head" or chief work, Great, Hauptwerk.

In the English organ, nomenclatures generally match those used in American organs. Additional names encountered are Orchestral organ and Tuba organ.

It would be difficult, not to say unrealistic, to hope to memorize the material of this chapter. It is intended largely as explanatory material and for handy reference in studying the music of various countries. The assignments following may, however, prove useful as selected by your instructor.

ASSIGNMENT

1) What confusion is likely to arise in following registration sugges-tions in American or English editions where manuals are indicated by number rather than by name?

2) In what country is the use of enclosed divisions considered particularly dispensable in organ design?

3) What are Antiphonal and Bombarde organs?

[1] Fernando Germani, *Method for the Organ* (Rome: Edizioni de Santis, 1953), Book I, Part IV, p. 22.

4) What is the meaning of the following: Hauptwerk, Oberwerk, Rückpositiv, Schwellwerk?

5) Define these manual nomenclatures: Grand Orgue, Positif, Récit.

6) In the Spanish organ, the Cadireta is located where?

7) Were Italian organs noted for the number and variety of their manual divisions?

8) Give German equivalents of the following Dutch nomenclatures: Groot Manuaal, Rugpositief, Hoofd Manuaal, Onderwerk.

13

THE EXPRESSION PEDALS

Numerous sources suggest that invention of the organ swell box can be attributed to an Englishman named Jordan in the year 1712, although other experiments had definitely been made along this line. It is obvious that a great bulk of organ literature written before and after this date and including the monumental output of the organ's greatest master composer, J. S. Bach, can and should be played without use of the one or more expression or swell pedals. Why, then, go to the expense of isolating one or more divisions of the organ in rooms and somewhat inhibiting the speech of the pipes by separating them from the room into which they are to speak by a wall of louvers that can be opened and closed to give a gradual increase or decrease of volume of tone without the addition of stops? The answer is a simple one.

Many composers have conceived their music with such gradations of tone level in mind, and proper performance of their music demands use of the expression pedal(s). The romantic period in general has given us organ literature demanding such subtlety of expression as this device affords. The nineteenth-century French school in particular, the music of Karg-Elert, and of certain contemporary English and American composers is not easily rendered on many organs of Germany, for instance, where some instruments are still constructed in which no single division is "under expression." The essential problem for the new student is to decide first where the use of the expression pedal(s) can be artistically made. Does the music call for such effects? Is this effect consistent with the period and style of the music? If the music is Bach, the answer is decidedly "no," unless the instrument is so small as to render addition of stops alone unsatisfactory to the achievement of the rising dynamic requirements of a given composition. If they *must* be used here, the swell boxes had better be opened in moments of rest where no accordion-like effect will result. Earlier writers suggest a very slow opening of the swell box for the same reason, the very nature of a Bach fugue with its relentless drive often precluding use of rests for opening the boxes. Since Bach had terraced dynamics in mind as a primary source of contrast and a gigantic final climax— such as one often hears in romanticized performances—with all manuals coupled was not necessarily required in his music, you should reflect duly and carefully before you make any use of the swell shutters in Bach's music, other than to open them and leave them open throughout a composition. Surely the muffled tone of a division with swell shutters completely closed is a tonal effect foreign to true Bach style and a questionable expediency even in "extenuating circumstances."

The slow movements of Mendelssohn's sonatas can be helpful in learning the use of the swell pedal. In addition to the two manuals normally required, subtle use of the expression pedals can add greatly to the musical effect. The writer has noted that in some editions the markings given by editors, followed too closely, can result in a caricature of the simple, straightforward character of this music. With the help of your instructor, you must decide where and how much you can use the swell pedal.

Both feet not only can but should be brought into play as pedal-ling allows. This must be carefully decided and practiced from the moment all correct notes, fingering, and pedalling have been achieved. Sometimes one continuous swell can be achieved by first a tap on the expression pedal (s) with one foot and then the other, as pedalling demands a change of feet.

Most secure control of the swell mechanism is achieved by placing the foot so that it is entirely on the pedal in a firm position. Here it can be opened by pressure of the toes or closed by pressure of the heel. Two adjacent expression pedals can be operated by placing the foot on the line between the two at once. Swell boxes can be quickly closed, also, by a sudden pressure of the toes at the *bottom* of the swell pedal when time free from pedalling is limited.

14

REGISTRATION MECHANICS

In Chaps. 2 and 3 you were introduced to the accessories of the console, and Chap. 13 developed the use of the expression pedals. Additional suggestions for the use of the accessories are now in order.

The Crescendo Pedal

This pedal is seldom required; however, its main use is for music of romantic character where sudden or frequent dynamic changes make it desirable to the performer. Some consoles provide a series

53

of small indicator lights connected with the crescendo pedal; these come on at points in the graduated dynamic increase, or conversely, go off as the level of volume decreases. The gradual change of level of volume can be made quite easily and without use of pistons.

Limiting factors affecting the usefulness of the crescendo pedal are: (a) the inclusion of stops unwanted in classic or baroque literature, for example, rather soft stops and reeds of solo character; (b) the invariable arrangement, that is, order of addition of stops, built into the device does not suit artistic requirements of most organ literature; (c) the inclusion on old or poorly reconstructed instruments of a variety of stops, such as vox humana, echo stops, solo reeds, not suitable for *any* kind of ensemble.

On some present-day instruments in Germany a surprising flexibility has been built into the rollschweller (crescendo pedal). A row of controls with a switch for every stop in the organ allows for disengaging any unwanted stops from those to be added by the device. This means that the player can set up any desirable combination as his ultimate "full crescendo," but naturally he cannot change the *order* in which they can be added.

The music of Karg-Elert, Reger, or Sowerby, to name only three composers, offers the organist many opportunities for employment of the crescendo pedal.

The Sforzando Reversible

This control is normally used only in romantic or modern music. Some builders (for example, Schantz of Ohio) provide up to three such controls allowing for stages in securing full organ on sizeable instruments. Toe-stud controls are commonly featured with duplicate manual controls. The sforzando reaches full organ with inclusion of heavy reeds and some 16′ tone.

The Piston—Operation

A most useful and necessary accessory, giving the performer immeasurably greater control over his instrument than he could otherwise enjoy, is the piston. One type of piston in common use is (a) that which can be set at the console by pressing and holding the

54

piston to be set and, with slight pressure, putting on all stops required, at the same time taking off any not desired. The other type is known as (*b*) the capture system, recognizable by the presence of a *setter* control, often found on the lowest manual to the far left. To operate, merely set up the combination required (for individual manual, pedal, or general piston control), depress the setter button and *while holding this,* press the piston on which the combination you set manually is desired.

Certain advantages and disadvantages are to be found in either system. The capture system has a special adaptability in setting graduated ensemble combinations. First set your starting piston, such as, Swell No. 3; then, leaving that combination on, add the stops wished on No. 4; hold setter, press piston No. 4; now, to this combination, add stops for No. 5; hold setter and depress No. 5, and so on. You can set six to eight pistons in a few moments on this system, whereas on the other system, each stop must be depressed for addition on *each* successive piston.

Be careful in using the capture system that you depress the correct buttons in the correct order; otherwise you can (*a*) depress the wrong piston, necessitating correction of your error. Or, if piston to be set is not firmly pressed, (*b*) the proper change may not be made in the action. The first system is most often used on organs of small or medium size, although the Austin Organ Company incorporates it in its consoles, regardless of size, and finds it dependable.

Specific suggestions about the use of the piston in changing stops are given in other chapters. At this juncture a few general hints about the use of pistons may prove helpful.

The Piston—Effective Use

For efficient use of the system on any organ, a basic *plan* which can be applied to most any instrument is advisable. For example you can choose to employ Swell pistons as follows:

1-2 for very soft combinations (1 for flute céleste, 2 for string céleste)
3-6 for graduated ensemble combinations (beginning softly and building to full combination)
7-8 for special color requirements (reed solos, chimes)

Naturally the number of pistons varies with each organ, and you may find in the first half of a program you wish to play that you have early music in which no use can be made of some of the suggested combinations. The elimination of célestes would allow for more pistons for gradual ensemble buildup or other needed combinations.

The general pistons can be set in similar fashion:

1-2 for varied soft combinations
3-6 for ensemble buildup
7-8 for unusual color combinations (e.g., Sw. reed chorus plus mixture; Gr. full flue chorus for contrast)

This is only a suggested scheme which can be varied by the individual to suit his own needs. The important thing is to *have a system that will work for you.*

Selection of Pistons

Your choice of pistons may be governed by the requirements of the music being performed:

1. The position of the hands at a given moment in a given composition may dictate use of a particular hand and the most accessible piston for the thumb of that hand. Should this be an exception to your *usual* order for setting pistons, it is easy enough to remember as such.

2. Choice of a *toe piston* may be dictated by the continuous activity of the hands in a given work or section of a work. Where toe pistons are not available other expediencies may suffice: (*a*) use of crescendo pedal, if character of the music allows this; (*b*) use of an assistant to make changes—a "system" long in use since days when pistons were unknown and even today, especially in Europe on the continent, where sufficient mechanical controls are not present.

The Piston and Recital Preparation

In preparing pistons for use in a recital it is desirable to do as much as possible in advance of performance to eliminate loss of time for changes during the recital. Most organs have pistons adequate for at least half a recital without changes; necessary changes can then be made at intermission time. Since many times stops can be added or retired without pistons, particularly in early music, you can before the performance set not only pistons used for the first program group, but also pistons in excess of these should be set for your second group. The complexity of registration changes varies greatly from one piece to another and also from one period to another.

Even though you can set up registration by hand between movements, do not allow exceptional time to pass in this process. Often too long a break can result in a poor effect. Some composers have proved their sensitivity to such periods of silence between movements by indicating specific periods of rest, or by employing terms like *enchainez* or *segue,* requiring the performer to begin playing the following movement as soon as rhythmic requirements of the present movement are met.

In making a note of pistons and their combinations, you will find the use of abbreviations helpful; make these as simple as possible in order to avoid ambiguity. Index cards serve well for this and can be used unobtrusively at the console. When playing from memory, you may find it helpful to use additional cards, listing required pistons *in sequence* as used in each work.

One useful scheme is to number general pistons and circle them:

①②. Manual pistons could be listed as $\boxed{\text{Sw. 1}}$, $\boxed{\text{So. 1}}$, meaning "Swell 1" and "Solo 1" respectively. The squares and circles, when marked in your music in ink, will allow for erasure of light pencil numbers, which will naturally be changed from time to time, unless you play from memory.

A system used in some organs in Europe is the numbering of *all* stops, couplers, and other controls. Registration can then be planned and recorded quickly using these numbers.

The changes required in every given work must be learned as surely as the notes for efficient, accurate performance. The plan of registration changes is, to the desired end of a satisfying performance, equally as important as the proper study and assimilation of a road map to one who wishes to reach his desired destination. In certain periods composers, such as Franck, have written into their music time for changes of stops, as well as a careful documentation of what these stops should be. Unfortunately, the absence or ambiguity of such indications is often a cause of much labor and study in order to know what actions are appropriate. Some points useful in dealing with these problems are given in discussions of the various schools of organ composition.

Above all, learn the requirements of each work: that is, the number and type of changes required, as well as the points where they occur. A few scratches in the margins of pages of a work are not enough. You should be able to recall the *plan* of changes for each work you are to perform so well that you can follow through its course in your mind, just as you can mentally "hear" a piece as it exists in time! If you do this habitually, you will be able to sit down and *register* almost any work without turning the first page of the music. Actual documentation of the *number* of changes will prove a helpful point for the beginning of this training.

The Unison Off

A device particularly useful on small organs is the unison off coupler. Although a few uses have been noted elsewhere, it may be well to stress here some applications of this coupler. In cancelling all stops of a given manual at their basic pitches, it allows you to secure stops at another pitch through the use of the sub or super coupler (s).

1. Under certain circumstances the Unison Off gives added flexibility in the use of divisions of an organ. For example, suppose you are playing a four-manual instrument in which the Positiv is located on the top manual. You could employ an ensemble on the Great, combining both Great and Choir (by using the Choir to Great 8′). Should you, at the same time, wish to play rapid echo passages, moving from the Great-Choir ensemble to another on the Positiv, it would be advantageous to couple the Positiv to Choir, and by cancelling the Choir (using the Unison Off on that manual), you could "move the Positiv" to the lowest manual, thus greatly

facilitating the rapid keyboard changes. The experienced player will find frequent uses for such changes.

2. Assume that on a small instrument your Swell reeds are trumpet 8′ and hautbois 4′. Obviously frequent use of the hautbois at 8′ pitch in solo work is advantageous. Rather than play the melody an octave lower than written, you can simply use both unison off and Swell to Swell 16′, thus altering the pitch of the hautbois to 8′. The builder has placed this reed at 4′ pitch so that it may be used as a complementary "chorus reed" with the trumpet 8′.

3. Assume that you have a small Choir on a romantic instrument. You may lack a single 2′ stop. A useful ensemble of 8′ and 2′ flutes can be secured by drawing the flute 4′, along with the unison off, Choir to Choir 16′, and Choir to Choir 4′. The unison off merely cancels the basic 4′ pitch of the flute, the sub-coupler produces a flute 8′ and the super-coupler, a flute 2′. Although it is not ideal to use two pitches from a single register (individual ranks can be contrasted in quality and therefore form a more complementary two-voice ensemble), the expediency can prove most useful on a small instrument.

4. In music of romantic character you might secure a fresh and colorful harmonic flute 8′ by combining a harmonic flute 4′, a reasonably common stop, with the unison off and the 16′ intramanual coupler.

Hand Registration

One of the most necessary techniques to develop for successful organ playing is hand registration: the addition or subtraction of stops accomplished without use of pistons. This can be learned from an early stage in the study of the instrument, and must be pursued until complete confidence in the execution of fairly difficult changes can be achieved. Basic to this practice is a knowledge of ensemble building. When you know how to add stops properly as required by a given composition, you can also retire the stops in the reverse order to which they have been added. A few suggestions are given toward the accomplishment of this skill.

ASSIGNMENT

1) Select a composition of homophonic character with the use of two different ensembles of moderate tone level. Work out this ensemble using the Sw. to Gr. 8′ coupler and both Sw. and Gr. 8′ couplers to Ped. Add a 16′ tone of moderate weight (e.g., bourdon), making sure that the Ped. combination balances with Gr., and, when the Gr. to Ped. 8′ is withdrawn, with Sw. Begin on the Gr. and later, where the character of the music allows, change to the Sw., at the same time taking off the Gr. to Ped. 8′ coupler. Where possible make the change manually. It is often possible to free one hand or the other, transferring one or two voices to the hand not being used to retire the coupler. If both hands are too busy to allow this, use the Gr. to Ped. reversible to make the change. Such a change can be made at an early stage in your organ study. Try to find a piece where this is feasible, simply for the sake of the practice it affords. Such a work is the "Andante tranquillo" from Mendelssohn's *Sonata III*. Although this work can be successfully registered by using an independent pedal combination that balances with either of the two ensembles required, some practice in the use of manual to pedal reversibles is quite useful.

2) A work of more advanced character in which the pedal combination must be frequently changed is the "Allegro maestoso" from Mendelssohn's *Sonata V*. Open with a *forte* combination on the Gr. coupled to secondary manual; at M. 29 a relatively quieter combination, possibly Sw. or Ch., is reached with the arpeggiated figure in the l.h. Retain the melody in the r.h. on the Gr. and retire the Gr. to Ped. 8′ coupler. At M. 35 the hands are shifted, the l.h. taking the melody on the Gr., the r.h. going to the Ch. Four measures later at M. 39, both hands go to the Ch., and, during the rests in the pedal part (M. 38), the Gr. to Ped. 8′ is added to bring out the melody in M. 39. This system can be carried throughout the work.

With the appearance of the first theme in the dominant tonality at M. 62, go back to the Gr. with an increased combination. This can be achieved by adding stops at appropriate, strong rhythmic points anywhere from Ms. 55 to 62. If you began with full-sounding flues, it would be well to add reed tone at M. 62, perhaps having a pedal piston set to bring Ped. up to balance the Gr., during the last rest in the bass of M. 61. The l. h. can easily be freed, especially in Ms. 59, 60, and 61, for adding some stops without pistons.

3) For practice in retiring stops, set a full combination for the opening "Grave" of Mendelssohn's *Sonata II*. You will note that a reduction is

called for in the last six measures before the double bar at the "Adagio." Learn to play these at the outset with the r.h., then as the rests occur in the r.h., upper staff, retire stops successively with the l.h. It is possible to polish this so smoothly that you can reduce both Gr. and Sw., finally retiring the Sw. to Gr. 8', and changing the Sw. to a solo combination (possibly oboe 8'), thus achieving the complicated change without use of a single piston. Remember you must reduce the Ped. along with the manual combinations. As diapasons 4' and 8' are retired from the Gr., for example, you will want to retire diapasons 8' and 16' from the Ped., finally leaving the Ped. with a soft combination that will balance it with the soft accompanying figures that are taken in the "Adagio" by the l.h. This movement affords ample opportunity for the change of manuals. As the melody shifts to the l.h., it is best to shift manuals; e.g., in M. 7 of the "Adagio," the r.h. leaves off the melody and picks up the sixteenth-note figure on the Gr. (sometimes this works best on the third sixteenth, and sometimes on the fourth), freeing the l.h. to resume the melody with the quarter note *d* on the Sw. Similar changes are made in Ms. 15, 17, and 19.

At M. 32, on the fourth sixteenth, a countermelody enters as the highest voice. This should be taken on the Sw. with the fifth finger of the r.h. The remaining fingers of the r.h. can then continue (on the second beat) the previous soprano voice on the Gr., playing on the two manuals at once, until on the second quarter note of M. 33 the l.h. can take over all of the accompanying parts (following the return at this point to only two inner voices in the musical structure).

4) For a final exercise in hand registration, the "Fugue" of Mendelssohn's *Sonata II* serves well. Couple foundation stops (8' and 4') of the Gr. and Sw. Begin on the Gr., the swell box being open. Close the swell box in M. 38, gradually beginning to open it again in M. 57. A buildup of tone begins in M. 63. At this point, following the sequence of a fragment of the subject, the subject enters on the tonic in M. 67. You can add to the manual ensemble by using the l.h. on the third beats of Ms. 63 and 65. In M. 67 add, with Ped. piston, as the subject enters on the first beat. You may want to add again to the manual ensemble on beat three of M. 67. These manual additions in Ms. 63, 65, and 67 can be facilitated by taking all manual parts with the r.h. If you use three manuals throughout, the choir box could be kept closed until the measures preceding the climax reached at M. 77. In M. 76 take the manual parts with the r.h. and, with the l.h., add the reed chorus of the Sw. on the downbeat of M. 77. Further stops can be added by the l.h.

on the third beat of M. 83 (possibly Gr. mixture). On the second eighth of M. 92 add the Ped. trombone 16', any further resources desired for the completion being added on the first beat of M. 96. At that point the full resources of the Gr. and Sw. (and Ch.) ensemble flues, mixtures, and reeds should be reached, possibly adding the Gr. trumpet at that point.

Some of the changes mentioned here could reasonably be made more easily by a well-constructed crescendo pedal. The practice, however, afforded by registering the entire piece by hand will prove most valuable.

15

EARLY ITALIAN ORGAN MUSIC

Earliest accounts of Italian organs picture relatively small instruments containing a wide selection of principals of different pitches ranging from 16' to ½' and a few flutes usually 8' and 4', possibly 2 2/3' and 2'. For expressive passages a beating stop, slightly mistuned, was supplied which would be combined with the principale 8' to form a céleste. This was known as the *fiffaro*. Reeds were introduced as early as the sixteenth century; the most common one seemingly was the voce umana (vox humana), although Germani mentions also the tromba, cornamusa, and regale.[1]

Through the courtesy of Ernesto Meli, president of the Frescobaldi Society of Brescia, the writer had the privilege of playing one of the best ancient instruments in all of Italy—that built by Antegnati in 1581 in Brescia and presently standing in the Church of

[1] *Op. cit.*, pp. 9-10.

St. Giuseppi. Its tone is well defined, sweet, and clear, and since only a few ranks have been replaced since the date of construction and these made carefully according to scaling and pipe metal prescribed by Antegnati at the period of the organ's construction, it stands as a functioning example of fine early instruments.[2] The specifications appear as follows:

Principale	16'
Principale spezzato	16'[3]
Ottava	8'
Quintadecima	4'
Decima nona	2 2/3'
Vigesima seconda	2'
Vigesima sesta	1 1/3'
Vigesima nona	1'
Trigesima terza	2/3'
Altra Vigesima seconda	2'
Flauto in quintadecima	4'
Flauto in ottava	8'

The importance of this organ and its preservation is increased when we realize that Constanzo Antegnati who built it left a list of specific suggestions for proper registration based on its specifications. The second 2' stop is a flute for use in "concertizing." Suggestions made by Antegnati are as follows:

A medium combination or mixture included principals of 16', 8', 1', and 2/3'
Principale 16', Ottava 8', Flauto 8'
Principale 16', Flauto 8'
Ottava 8', Decima nona 2 2/3', Flauti 8' and 2' (cornet effect)
Ottava 8', Flauto 8' (for polyphonic passages or those containing ornamentation)
Ottava 8', Flauto 8', and tremulant (for sustained music)
Principale 16' (suitable for the elevation)
The two 16' principali
Flauto 8'

[2] The instrument was restored in 1955.
[3] A divided stop, the upper portion being used for manual, the lower, for pedal.

Principale (manual part of the spezzato rank), Flauto 8'
Principale 16', Flauto 4'
Principale 16', Flauto 4, plus Ottava 8'

Ripieno is a term equivalent to the German *Werk* or *Hintersatz*. It meant a full-organ sound employing all stops of the principal chorus, excepting the Principale spezzato, and excluding flutes. The Italian preference for drawing ranks of the mixture separately is logical enough when we realize that the one-manual instrument was the norm, and such a procedure gave great flexibility. The term *"ripieno"* means "filling up," obviously used in a most functional sense.

A few basic conclusions can be drawn from study of the foregoing information. Flutes were ordinarily omitted from relatively full ensemble combinations. For special effect there was no hesitation to duplicate pitches or to mix tonal families. Sixteen-foot manual tone can be employed (a) for full effects (where it is normally balanced with ample high registers), or (b) where gravity or solemnity of tone is desired. Other suggested combinations for rapid passage work are:

Principale 16', Altra Vigesima seconda 2'
The above, with Ottava 8'
Principale 16', Ottava 8', Flauto 2 2/3'

At the beginning of the seventeenth century Girolamo Diruta published an important work *Il Transilvano* which contained, among other things, a detailed list of suggestions for stop combinations suited to the character of the twelve ecclesiastical modes.[4]

I.	Dorian	Principale 16', Ottava 8' Vigesima seconda 2', Flauto 4' (optional)	dignified
II.	Hypodorian	Principale 16', tremulant	melancholy
III.	Phrygian	Principale 8', Flauto 8'	mournful
IV.	Hypophrygian	Principale 16', tremulant	gloomy

4 Dates vary, however, based on best available information it seems that the two parts of this work were published in 1597 and 1609.

V.	Lydian	Ottave 8', Flauto 4',	
		Quinta decima 4'	happy
VI.	Hypolydian	Principale 16', Ottava 8'	
		Flauto 4'	devotional
VII.	Mixolydian	Ottava 8', Quinta decima 4',	
		Vigesima seconda 2'	lively
VIII.	Hypomixolydian	Flauto 8'; or Ottava 8' and	
		Flauto 8'; or Flauto 8' and	
		Vigesima seconda 2'	agreeable
IX.	Aeolian	Principale 16', Quinta decima	
		4', Vigesima seconda 2'	pleasant
X.	Hypoaeolian	Principale 16' with either	
		Ottava 8' or Flauto 8'	somber
XI.	Ionian	Flauto 8'; or Flauto 8' and	
		Quinta decima 4'; or Flauto 8'	
		and Vigesima seconda 2'; or	
		Ottava 8', Quinta decima 4'	
		and Vigesima seconda 2'	lively
XII.	Hypoionian	Ottava 8', Flauto 8', and	
		Vigesima seconda 2'	lively [5]

Forms

Proper registration procedures rest on a knowledge of forms exploited by writers of the Italian school. The verse (*verso*, plural *versi*), written for use by the organist in alternation with sung portions of the mass, is here encountered. These short pieces are often of a moving character and present no problem of registration changes in their course.

The large forms characteristic of the school are the *ricercare, canzona,* toccata, and fantasia. The *ricercare* and fantasia are close cousins, both featuring imitative development of material, a style characteristic that evolved as a result of the writing techniques brought to Italy by the composers of Flanders. The fantasia, as suggested by its title, was a piece in which considerable freedom was

[5] Sources vary slightly in rendering this information about Diruta's registration suggestions. See E. Harold Geer, *Organ Registration in Theory and Practice* (Glen Rock, N. J.: J. Fischer & Bro., 1957), p. 234; Germani, *op. cit.*, p. 10; or Gerald Stares Bedbrook, *Keyboard Music from the Middle Ages to the Beginnings of the Baroque* (London: Macmillan & Co., Ltd., 1949), p. 72.

taken with working out of material. The *ricercare* (from the verb meaning "to search out" or "to find special effects") was a complex contrapuntal work in which devices such as inversions, augmentations and diminutions, proportional rhythms, and the like appear.

In the *canzona,* a composition growing out of early paraphrases of French songs, we find an ancestor of the fugue, featuring the use of imitative material with answers often at the intervals commonly expected in the fugue. The "song" character is often apparent in this work, and since the time (sixteenth century) when Girolamo Cavazzoni first introduced a section in 3/2 time into a work in common time, this particular rhythmic device has become a frequent characteristic of the form. It is worth passing note that G. Cavazzoni was the son of a celebrated organist of Rome and Venice, Marcantonio Cavazzoni, and in turn, teacher of Costanzo Antegnati, the famous organ builder.

Despite the fact that today the toccata is often considered an excellent piece for display of the performer's talents, we find many examples in the early school of Italy of quiet or devotional character. Specifically the form is a work for keyboard, as the verb from which it is drawn means "to touch." It also means "to knock or beat," as in playing a drum! An ancestor of the instrumental prelude, the toccata often did have considerable passage work.

Registration of the foregoing forms must be consistent with their sectional character; that is, changes must coincide with either a double bar separating the parts of the work or with strong rhythmic changes in their basic character. Other helpful aspects of interpretation of such pieces can be found in the preface, which that master of the Italian baroque who brought numerous forms to perfection, Girolamo Frescobaldi, wrote in his *Musical Flowers (Fiori Musicali)*. He gave suggestions for freedom in rhythmic treatment that come as a great surprise to most upon first reading. He advised free use of rubato for expressive passages, stating that trills are to be taken freely, without hurry, giving a slight pause on the last note of "the shakes or passages." He admonished the use of retard at the end of sections with plenty of time for cadences.[6] He even advised starting toccatas slowly in order that acceleration can be

[6] Bedbrook, *op. cit.,* p. 126.

achieved gradually. It is not amiss, Frescobaldi said, to stop at any point convenient or simply to play any part of a large composition that suits the performer's needs. This might have proved convenient in the light of the fact that we read a bell was sometimes provided to warn the organist who let himself get carried away and play too long.

Obviously large organ resources are not required for proper performance of Frescobaldi's music, but securing the proper sounding stops may at the same time only be achieved with ease on a large instrument. Only those stops voiced in the gentle character of earlier Italian principals and flutes should be employed. If diapasons are too gamba-like or are scaled to sound extremely heavy, they cannot well convey the desired effect. Germani suggests that the use of flute mutations can give the variety in pitch and character often desired, and substitution of a flute 8′, especially if the character is not far removed from that of a principal, for a too heavy diapason 8′ may achieve good results.[7] Mixtures that tend to shriek would, also, not be in character. Stops of pronounced string quality should be avoided, as well as string célestes, modern reeds like the clarinet, or chorus reeds of any degree of weight. As the Principale 16′ was available only occasionally on early Italian organs, it can well be omitted unless its character is suitably light and clear.

The early Italian organ first had pedals of a pulldown type, where manual pipes were sounded by a device attached by rope beneath the keys of the lower manual. Independent pedals were developed and stops alloted to that division in the seventeenth century.[8] The nondiatonic construction along with the fact that these pedals, being quite short, were played only with the toes emphasizes the sparing use of pedal notes. An examination of the early music where extensive pedal parts have not been given by editors, will show that the composer spaced his music in such a way that all important melodic lines could be played by hands alone. An occasional long tone or a few important cadential notes might, then, have sufficed in the Pedal department. Where pedal *is* employed for the convenience and

[7] *Op. cit.,* p. 11.
[8] *Ibid.,* p. 9.

ease of performance, its character should not be more weighty than that of the manual—unless, of course, it is employed in the manner mentioned above, for an occasional important note, where there can be more contrast in color and character.

Certain exceptions to the above, based on careful analysis of actual sounds, can be made. The writer feels that modern solo reeds may well be used, if, like the English horn, they give a tone not widely different from the early solo reeds of the schnarrwerk category. A reed with well-blending mutation(s) may serve for a solo voice. If a melody lies in a very high register, reed tone is not likely to be suitable; flute or principal tone is preferable.

Although contrasts can be achieved through change of manual, it is well to take care to avoid excessive "hacking up" of a composition intended to be, quite often, an unfoldment of a single idea presented in various guises. In a sense, the refinement exhibited in the works must be carried out in registration, along with obvious rhythmic subtleties, in order to render these great works as they were intended to be rendered.

16

FRENCH ORGAN MUSIC

Jean Titelouze (1563-1633) is considered the father of French organ music. In his time the presence of two manuals and pedal was an accepted convention in French organ building. As in Italy the pedal had as its early function an *en tirasse* arrangement; that is, the pedals were used to pull down the keys of the manual above through a coupling mechanism. Pedal parts were largely limited to the performance of *cantus firmus* melodies in such an instrument.

Sixteenth-Century Stops

Stops in common usage from the sixteenth century included:

diapasons (montre, prestant, doublette)
bourdons (equivalent to stopped flute, gedeckt)
open flutes
mixtures of ensemble (both grave and acute) and solo types
reeds of ensemble and solo character and of both long (bombarde, trompette) and short (voix humaine, cromorne) resonator categories

The Pedal

We note that the Pedal division of an organ designed by Titelouze contained flutes 8′ and 4′ and trumpet 8′. Some writers feel that these were borrowed stops. In any case, it is evident that their usage was for melodic lines, often simply the playing of a *cantus firmus* melody, and they were not expected to enter into any sort of polyphonic and complicated texture as was expected of the Pedal divisions of the organs of north Germany. It is noteworthy that no 16′ stops are indicated, and the basic pitch of the Pedal was 8′ or the same as that of the Positif (that of the Grand Orgue was 16′). Germani suggests that the state of the French pedal board remained most "uninviting" and gave little encouragement for the development of pedal technique until it underwent transformation under the influence of Boely in 1836! [1]

In the seventeenth century additional manuals appeared, leading eventually to as many as five; but the extra manuals were for solo or special effect, and did not affect the organization of the two basic manuals.

[1] *Op. cit.,* p. 47.

The Grand Orgue and Positif

Composition of the Grand Orgue (Great) and Positif (unenclosed Choir) was similar, but the voicing of the Grand Orgue was the bolder of the two and it contained a 16′ (montre and/or bourdon). There were diapasons of 8′, 4′, and 2′, and commonly each contained both fourniture and cymbale. Note the contrast to the Italian organ design where the compound stops were absent and buildup of tone could be created gradually. Bourdons of 16′ (Grand Orgue), 8′, and 4′ were common, as well as flutes of many different pitches, including mutations. The presence of bright 8′ and 4′ reeds, as well as solo reeds (régale, voix humaine, and cromorne) completed the picture with the cornet, most commonly used for solo purposes but also combined with ensembles containing reeds.

Early Récit, Bombarde, and Echo

Additional manuals, added in the seventeenth and eighteenth centuries, included the Récit (generally compared to the Swell but in early instruments really a small Solo), the Bombarde, and the Echo. It was common practice to furnish an entire manual for only one or two stops. The Récit often contained no more than a cornet and a trompette in early organs. The Echo might contain only a cornet or cornet and voix humaine. Stops intended for use as solos in certain registers often ran less than the full compass of Positif and Grand Orgue, although for obvious reasons of symmetry in instrument design a complete keyboard would nonetheless be provided. For example, in the Rouen Cathedral organ, built in 1689 by Cliquot, the two main manuals each had a fourty-eight-note compass; the Récit, only twenty-five; and the Echo, thirty-seven. This same instrument, by the way, had no independent Pedal stops (though an instrument of forty-one stops) and only a coupler from Grand Orgue to Pedale.[2] On the Nôtre Dame organ in Paris, built in 1733, the Bombarde organ contained reeds as follows: 16′, 8′, 8′, and 4′. It had also a Grand Cornet of five ranks, both Fourniture and Cymbale, a Montre 32′, and Bourdon 16′.[3]

[2] *Ibid.,* p. 55.
[3] *Ibid.,* p. 56.

70

Coupling

Coupling was possible from Positif or Bombarde to Grand Orgue. This was done by the pulling out of the Bombarde so that projections below the keys of the upper manual depressed those of the lower. In similar manner the Positif could be pushed in so that its keys would be depressed by projections below the keys of the Grand Orgue.[4]

It is proper to assume that coupling was not common or, if employed, it did not generally bring into play full Grand Orgue and Positif ensembles at one time, since wind supply was not sufficient to allow for successful performance on such a combination.[5]

Arrangement of the Manuals Varied

The position of Positif and Grand Orgue was sometimes reversed. Ordinarily the following was characteristic of early instruments:

I. Positif, II. Grand Orgue, III. Récit, (IV. Echo)

I. Positif, II. Grand Orgue, III. Clavier de Bombarde, IV. Récit, V. Echo

The Tremulant

A mistaken notion is that the tremulants are inappropriate for early music. The French organs were usually supplied with two—a mild one and a stronger one—and we read somewhat hair-raising accounts of early organists who called for full or brilliant combinations *with* tremolo! We also read that the tremolo was a stop much used and abused, and we can well assume this to be an instance of abuse.

Baroque Registration Conventions

Finally, we come down to a precise set of rules as repeated in numerous works, the conventions of registration which became ac-

[4] Geer, *op. cit.*, p. 246.
[5] Germani, *op. cit.*, p. 48.

cepted in French baroque practice. Some of the most important are
as follow:

(Principal Chorus)

Grand plein jeu: diapasons 16′ to 2′, (sometimes bourdons), fourniture, and cymbale.

Petit plein jeu: the same as the above (except for the 16′) but on
Positif. (Various writers suggest combination of reeds 8′ and 4′
or reeds in the pedal only with the plein jeu. It seems likely,
however, that the plein jeu was intended to be a combination
omitting reed stops, at least on the manuals.)

Reed Chorus

Grand jeu: bourdons and flutes including mutations, cornet, prestant
4′, and trompettes 8′ and 4′ (Grand Orgue).

Petit jeu: the same as the above but on Positif. (Where trompette
8′ and clairon 4′ were absent, the cromorne—sometimes used for
ensemble purposes—could logically be substituted. In the case of
a modern instrument, the clarinet is a poor substitute, however.)

Grand jeu de tièrce: bourdons and flutes, 16′ to higher octaves and
mutations, the *tièrce.* (On occasion the montre 8′ and/or prestant
4′ are required.)

Petit jeu de tièrce: the same as above but on Positif. (Some writers
suggest that duplications be omitted here.)

These basic combinations are often encountered. Some writers suggest that the tièrce should be omitted from reed combinations but, as
the cornet contains the seventeenth and this stop is required for the
grand jeu, we have reason to suspect that the omission should apply
only to small combinations indended for chordal style. Germani
notes that the *grand jeu* was used "to reinforce the reed harmonics." [6]
We know that the cymbale is on occasion constructed with third-
sounding ranks, to which the ear is somewhat tolerant due to the
very high pitches involved; it is reasonable that even in some early
organs tièrce ranks might have been used in ensemble mixtures.
Admittedly most mixtures constructed for use in ensemble contain
only octave- and fifth-sounding ranks.

[6] *Ibid.,* p. 49.

Forms

Structure Denoted by Nomenclatures
and Forms Named from Required Stops

With some knowledge of the early French organs we may turn to a study of forms used in the music of the times. In France, as in Spain, many early compositions were named from their structure or the stops required for their performance. Good examples are:

"*Récit de Cornet*": a recitative-like melody on the cornet with or without the addition of soft flues.

"*Récit de Cromhorne*": cromhorne with prestant 4', possibly bourdon 8' and nasard 2 2/3'.

"*Récit de Nasard*": flutes from 8' upward including nasard but omitting tièrce.

"*Basse de Trompette*": trompette 8' with prestant 4', possibly clairon 4'—a melody played in the lower register. (Nivers occasionally calls for cornet.[7])

"*Basse et Dessus de Trompette*": combination as above but a melody designed to exploit the treble (*dessus*) as well as bass register.

"*Fonds*": all foundations (flues) of 8' and 4'.

"*Fond doux*": As above omitting diapasons. Literally "sweet" or gentle foundation stops. Also "*jeu doux*."

It is noteworthy that the term "Récit" has a dual usage: as a manual nomenclature or as a descriptive term applied to a flowing, sometimes highly ornamented line. Considering the use of the Récit division for the performance of a piece of this character, the application is particularly consistent.

Fugues

Fugues or works of fugal character which contain considerable material of homophonic or accompanying character, such as, "Fantaisie" by Louis Couperin, figure extensively in early French music; although with rare exceptions none of the composers of the school

[7] Almonte C. Howell, Jr. (ed.), *Five French Baroque Organ Masses* (Lexington: University of Kentucky Press, 1961).

nears the peak of perfection in this field of writing that characterized the school culminating in Bach's music. Writers indicated numerous approaches to the registering of fugues from which a few general conclusions can be drawn: (*a*) The relatively brief works required no change of stops for their proper performance. (*b*) The character of the music itself must be considered in adopting a brilliant combination with considerable weight, or a bright but light combination for lively fugues. Some possibilities might be:

For a stately fugue:

a) grand jeu and petit jeu (without cornets)
b) the same, with montre 8′

For a lively fugue:

a) grand jeu ~~Reed Chorus~~
b) jeu de tièrce (Grand Orgue or Positif)

Homophonic Music

Many pieces written in this period were devoid of imitation or other contrapuntal techniques. These, too, are often named for their combinations. An example would be the "Grand Jeu" of DuMage. The more massive and chordal the effect in a given composition, the more care you must take to avoid any undue impression of hurry in performance. The middle section of the DuMage work might be performed with some reduction of tone; and where repetitions occur near the close of the middle section you can make use of two secondary manuals, Positif and Echo, or possibly Récit and Echo. A return to slower tempo and the original, massive effect is indicated in the final section.

Another such piece is the "Fond d'Orgue" of Marchand or the "Point d'Orgue Sur Les Grands Jeux" by Nicolas de Grigny.

Echos and Dialogues

Dramatic alterations of manuals are featured in works simply entitled "Echo"—a technique favored by the great master, Sweelinck, of the Netherlands. Contrasts of dynamic level are featured, as well as contrasts of texture and color. Grand Orgue and Positif can be used as in the "Dialogue" by Marchand.

Similar treatment can be used to advantage in "Les Cloches" ("The Bells") by LeBégue—a charming piece developing a four-note ground motive.

You can begin on the Positif with the first augmentation of the opening ostinato figure being taken on the Grand Orgue at M. 8, all parts going to Grand Orgue on M. 14 for three measures, with return to Positif, and so on. With the appearance of the double augmentation of the ostinato figure in M. 28, use Grand Orgue and Pedal. The short "middle division" starting at M. 48 should be played on strongly contrasted Récit, followed by single-measure alternations with Echo, starting on the second beat of M. 53; change back to alternating Positif and Grand Orgue beginning in M. 58.

A good example of the echo technique can be seen in the "Concert pour les Flutes" from the Gloria of the "Mass on the Eighth Tone" by Gaspard Corrette. In the same mass is a "Dialogue à deux Choeurs," featuring alternation of grand jeu and petit jeu. Also the offertory, "Grand Dialogue à Trois Choeurs," has sections using this same technique as well as other techniques, such as, dividing the hands to play on different manuals and using (as suggested by the title) a third level of volume (Echo). In the Gloria of this mass is a "Dialogue de Voix humaine," illustrating the fact that a solo is sometimes featured in a melodic passage (sometimes left hand, sometimes right) against jeu doux.

Récits

A very sizeable category of pieces involves the recitative melodic technique—a flowing, highly ornamented melody against a homophonic accompaniment. The location of the melody, whether a soprano (*en dessus*), a tenor (*en taille*), or a bass (*en basse*), as well as the name of the required combination for its execution, figures in the titles. Examples are:

"*Basse de Trompette*," Nivers, Marchand
"*Tièrce en Taille*," Marchand

75

"Basse et Dessus de Trompette," Clérambault
"Récit de Cromhorne," Nivers
"Cromhorne en Taille," Corrette
"Récits de Cromhorne et de Cornet separé," Clérambault

The last composition features two solo combinations instead of a single solo line, with flues used as a foil. The "Cornet separé" (literally, "a mounted cornet") is so named because it was placed alone on an elevated chest to enhance its tonal effect. The Récit combinations above do not necessarily imply single registers, even where a reed is required. For instance, the trompette when in lower register might well be reinforced with the clairon 4′ or prestant 4′ or perhaps both. The voix humaine might have a flute 8′ or 4′ or even a prestant 4′ added. To the cromorne might be added a flute 8′ or 4′. It is not unreasonable to suppose that a mutation of lower pitch, such as the nasard, when in suitable register could reinforce a solo reed. It is noteworthy that the nasard is not generally called for in low-pitched melodies unless combined with ample unison and octave registers due to its tendency to overshadow and obscure the basic pitch when a melody reaches into lower tenor and bass registers. The use of a reed with nasard would not be as subject to this difficulty as flute with nasard due to the fact that reeds do not lose their incise and penetrating tone in low registers where a flute of 8′ pitch becomes increasingly ambiguous in character.

Duos, Trios, Quatuors

The last category, excepting the important masses wherein all manner of techniques are employed, is that including duos, trios, and quatuors, in which effort is made to isolate and emphasize the individual character of lines. *Duos* are likely to be lively pieces with bright combinations required for their execution (cornets, trompette). In the *trio,* as often as not, we find two voices played on one manual against one on another; due to the rudimentary nature of pedal parts in general, a part conceived for Pedal would have to require a lower level of technical development than available on a manual. The advantage of the higher part (s) in the brightness of register is often offset by using a slightly louder combination for a low voice. In the *quatuor* it is common to find two parts on one manual, a third on another, with Pedal serving for the fourth; but genuine four-division quatuors are to be found. One might note in passing that Marchand was one of the earliest writers to call for overlapping lines in Pedal (short double-pedal parts), and in these cases no 16′ tone would be expected.

The Organ Mass

As suggested above the movements of a mass may require many techniques of registration already discussed. Whereas the organ masses of the Attaignant collections (1528-29) are largely made up of somewhat abstract compositions, usually in motet style and reflecting the spirit and style of the Renaissance, also often employing the plainsong of the mass as a basis, the works of the baroque period show a strong secular influence and a keen interest in exploiting the tonal resources of their instrument.

The organ mass developed into a structure as follows: the organ played the first verset of the mass, choir followed with the second, and the alternation continued throughout the proper of the mass with the exception that, understandably, the Credo was left intact. Additional pieces were furnished for such service requirements as the Gradual, Elevation, Communion, and the Offertory. Here composers often seemed to feel free to write more expansively than in the proper of the mass, and some lovely movements are the result. It is curious that a few masses have versets so extensive as to make us wonder if they, like the Bach "B Minor Mass" (obviously too long to have a "practical" service use), were not composed as prime examples of the composer's ability, flowering as it could when not reduced to the everyday requirements of the service.

Variation Forms

In addition to the mass we find pieces in variation form that require more definite and frequent registration changes than shorter pieces. Three examples would be the "Chaconne Grave en Sol Majeur" of LeBégue, the "Laissez Paistre vos Bestes" of Nicolas Gigault, and the "Quand le Sauveur Jésus-Christ Fut Né de Marie" by Pierre Dandrieu.

77

Late Baroque

The builder whose work brought to a climax the principles of the French baroque organ art was Francois Henri Cliquot. Noted for his fine reeds, operated on small wind pressure and yet giving great brilliance with maximum blend in ensemble, Cliquot's organs were instruments of quality, some of which still stand in the restored organs of "St. Nicolas des Champs, St. Gervais, and St. Merry, in Paris." [8] It was for such an instrument as that which Cliquot built for St. Sulpice in Paris, 1781, that Dom Bédos wrote his important theoretical work, "The Art of the Builder of Organs" (four parts issued between 1766-78). Analysis of the components of the St. Gervais organ reveals the presence of two or more reeds on each manual and pedal, even the Echo having both Trompette 8′ and Clairon 4′. The Positif and Grand Orgue each have a number of mutations and mixtures, and all five manuals contain cornets. Specifications are:

Positif

Montre 8′	Bourdon 16′	Trompette 8′
Prestant 4′	Bourdon 8′	Clairon 4′
Doublette 2′	Flûte 4′	Cromorne 8′
Fourniture IV	Nasard 2 2/3′	Basson 8′
Cymbale V	Quarte de Nasard 2′	Clarinette 8′
	Tièrce 1 3/5′	
	Larigot 1 1/3′	
	Cornet V	

Grand orgue

Montre 32′	Bourdon 16′	Trompette 8′
Montre 16′	Bourdon 8′	Second Trompette 8′
Montre 8′	Flûte 8′	Clairon 4′
Prestant 4′	Tièrce 3 1/5′ [9]	Second Clairon 4′
Doublette 2′	Nasard 2 2/3′	
Fourniture IV	Quarte de Nasard 2′	

[8] William Leslie Sumner, *The Organ* (London: The Macmillan Co., Ltd., 1952), p. 202.

[9] This stop might conceivably belong to the category of the montre, but could also be for use with bourdons in a grand cornet combination.

Second Fourniture VI	Petite Tièrce 1 3/5'
Cymbale IV	Nasard 1 1/3'
	Cornet V

Bombarde	*Récit*	*Echo*
Cornet V	**Flûte 8'**	Bourdon 8'
Bombarde 16'	Cornet V	Flûte 4'
Bombarde 8'	Hautbois 8'	Cornet V
Clairon 4'	Trompette 8'	Trompette 8'
		Clairon 4'

Pédale

Flûte 16'	Bombarde 32'
Bourdon 16'	Bombarde 16'
Flûte 8'	Trompette 8'
Second Flûte 8'	Second Trompette 8'
Nasard 5 1/3'	Clairon 4'
Flûte 4'	

The French preference for two distinct categories of flutes, the stopped (Bourdon) type and the open (usually simply called Flûte) is here evidenced. Besides trompettes and bombardes, note the variety of reed color—Cromorne, Basson, Clarinette, Hautbois.

One interesting suggestion given by Dom Bédos is that a bourdon be used with a reed when the latter is too "edgy" in tone.[10] He mentions also the use of duplicate, soft 8' registers for accompanimental work; to gain volume, he says, add a Flûte 4', but never a 16'. The Prestant 4' he regards as too "sharp" in tone for accompanimental purposes.

The Romantic, "Orchestral" Organ

The next builder to change the face of the art in France was even more innovational in his approach than Cliquot had been. Aristide Cavaillé-Coll was born in 1811 to a family that could trace the organ-building tradition back for more than a century. Carrying on work initiated by Dominique, his father, Aristide developed a

[10] Sumner, *op. cit.,* p. 349.

1. "coupling pedal" by which an organist could transfer stops drawn on one manual to another, allowing for greater *crescendi* and *diminuendi* through this means, a practice that became and has remained common in the performance of romantic and modern French organ music.[11]

2. This concept of manual combination plus Cavaillé-Coll's new reed chorus, giving a blaze of color that *dominated* the entire ensemble, are possibly that builder's outstanding and most revolutionary practices. Ranking close to this was his concept of combining varied 8′ registers as a basic part of the ensemble—as opposed to the baroque idea of the basic principal chorus, with flute or bourdon

3. tone to be added for special purposes. Since none of these stops (Montre, Gambe, Flûte Harmonique, Bourdon) was unduly thick, all could be added in the ensemble. The resulting sound, when Fonds 8′ are demanded in French music, is an ensemble with breadth of tone not easily duplicated in American instruments of small size.

Cavaillé-Coll introduced reeds of orchestral quality, allowing some of these to replace old, short resonator reeds; for example, the clarinet replaced the cromorne. He felt that mutations were most

4. useful in creating complex-color effects and in imitating orchestral color on the organ. Sumner notes that the Septieme 4 4/7′, placed in the Pedal at Nôtre Dame, gave a quality to the flue work that Vierne characterized as a sound like that of "a muster of double-basses." [12]

5. Another innovation was the enlarging of the Récit to a sizeable division under control of an expression pedal. It is worthy of note that in 1875 he enclosed the Positif, thus giving a second expressive division.[13] Even so, the romantic, orchestral effect to be gained through use of the "new" instrument here described dictated coupling of Récit to Positif and both of these to Grand Orgue. With such a system all manuals were affected by a single Récit expressive division.

Mixtures remained important in Cavaillé-Coll's work, and these with the reed choruses gave his instruments striking, dramatic ensembles.

[11] *Ibid.,* p. 209.
[12] *Ibid.,* p. 211.
[13] *Ibid.,* p. 214.

Franck

The earliest composer of importance to make full use of the new symphonic organ was César Franck (1822-90), who, though born in Belgium, achieved fame in France where he was organist at the great St. Clotilde for the last thirty-one years of his life. Here in 1859 Cavaillé-Coll installed an organ with the following specifications:

Grand orgue	Positif
Montre 16'	Bourdon 16'
Bourdon 16'	Montre 8'
Montre 8'	Gambe 8'
Gambe 8'	Flûte Harmonique 8'
Flûte Harmonique 8'	Bourdon 8'
Bourdon 8'	Salicional 8'
Prestant 4'	Prestant 4'
Octave 4'	Flûte Octaviante 4'
Quinte 2 2/3'	Quinte 2 2/3'
Doublette 2'	Doublette 2'
Plein Jeu V	Plein Jeu III
Bombarde 16'	Trompette 8'
Trompette 8'	Clarinette 8'
Clairon 4'	Clairon 4'

Récit	Pedale
Bourdon 8'	Quintaton 16'
Flûte Harmonique 8'	Contrebasse 16'
Viole de Gambe 8'	Flûte 8'
Voix Céleste 8'	Octave 4'
Flûte Octaviante 4'	Bombarde 16'
Octavin 2'	Basson 16'
Trompette 8'	Trompette 8'
Basson-Hautbois 8'	Clairon 4'
Voix Humaine 8'	
Clairon 4'	

enlarging the Récit.

Mechanics of the Romantic Organ

And now we come to the important mechanical details which must be known by the performer to understand clearly both the music of Franck and others who have written for the symphonic

French instrument, as well as how best to perform this music on organs of different character. The arrangement of manuals on Cavaillé-Coll's instruments was as follows: Grand Orgue, Positif, Récit, Bombarde or Echo. Comparing this with previous manual placement details in other organs, you will see that the position of the Grand Orgue and Positif varies, and sometimes the Bombarde is located as third manual. Cavaillé-Coll built additional mechanical controls into his instrument that, though they seem crude to the American organist today, were a great improvement, allowing the player to gain a new mastery over the organ. These included lock-down pedal couplers operating numerous controls:

Couplers from each manual to pedal (the *tirasses*).

Couplers from each upper manual to Grand Orgue.

Couplers called *ventils.* These were controls which permitted the sounding of reeds and upper work, placed on separate chests from the remaining work of a division. There were ventils for each manual division as well as pedal.

Grand Orgue *main ventil.* This had the effect of a unison intra-manual coupler and allowed the organist to perform any division(s) from the bottom manual, with or without drawn stops of the Grand Orgue. It also allowed for the coupling of any combination of manuals by playing them on the Grand Orgue.

Grand Orgue *subcoupler.* Particularly useful in performing music placed approximately in a range above middle *c*, this control helped bridge the gap between that ensemble and the pedal, producing a grand and full-sounding combination. This worked as subcoupler on any other manual coupled to Grand Orgue as well as on the Grand Orgue itself.

A Récit to Positif coupler.

Pedals controlling tremolos.

Significantly these were all built to be operated by the feet. The placement of stops of the consoles on terraces running out from either side of the manuals from which they are operated (leading to curved stop terraces in large instruments) made them particularly difficult to control. The composer, then, had to write his music so that few or no stop changes were necessitated while playing. It must be noted that the use of the ventils to control certain stops, particularly the reeds, allowed for pulling out these stops and actually bringing them into play by a single motion of the foot. This explains why music of French composers often calls for adding "The Reeds of the Swell" or "The Reeds of the Positif."

Sizeable organs contain yet another mechanical advantage, the *registres de combinaison*—ventil knobs placed on the stop terraces adjacent to the keyboards they affect. These can be used to admit or shut off the wind of the draw-stop mechanisms. When these knobs are not drawn, the stops cannot speak; hence no changes will have any effect. The organist prepares his changes as follows:

1. Ventil knobs are drawn.
2. Stops for the first combination desired are drawn.
3. Ventil knobs are then retired, locking the set combinations.
4. A second combination can now be prepared on the knobs.
5. These combinations can be brought on at will by the organist simply by drawing the ventil knobs again.

As mentioned previously the ventils of the *anches* allow for bringing on groups of predetermined combinations; in this case the action is accomplished though admitting wind to the reed soundboards. Generally when you see the word "anches" in music, especially with reference to a great volume of sound, the indication is for addition of reeds, but this may not necessarily be so. The organist may wish to draw mutations and/or mixtures as indicated above (the sounding of which is subject to the depressing of the ventil pedal), and reeds can be added later by the ventil knobs when also prepared as noted above.

Registration of Franck's Music

The registration of Franck's music is not especially problematic on a sizeable instrument. One factor likely to be troublesome is the indication "Fonds de 8'." As noted in Franck's organ, this could

[handwritten margin notes: Montre 8', Gambe 8', Bourdon 8', Flut Harmonique 8']

suggest addition of as many as four 8' stops, not always possible on American organs, and in such cases the broad effect desired cannot well be achieved, for a rohrflöte 8' or bourdon 8' combined with a geigenprinzipal 8' or diapason 8' does not exactly equal Franck's combination on the Grand Orgue, namely, Montre, Gambe, Flûte Harmonique, and Bourdon—all 8' stops.

When the term "Fonds" is encountered, it generally refers to stops of 8' and 4' combined. If deviations are desired (for example, Fonds de 8' et 16'), the required pitches are specified by the composer.

On an American instrument the organist may find his combination lacking in brilliance as compared to that of Cavaillé-Coll's organ in special cases. Where Trompette 8' and Clairon 4' are noted, perhaps to be combined with Jeu de Fonds, the resulting sound on the French instrument will be quite brilliant due to the quality of the reeds which, as we noted, tend to dominate any combination. If the reeds at hand are dull or lacking in harmonic development (for instance, a tuba or cornopean—reeds of smooth character) as compared to the French reed, it may prove helpful to draw a grave mixture to rectify the resulting dull combination. Experience, study of the music, listening to as many recordings made on French instruments as possible—all of these prove helpful in developing your judgment, for simply drawing equivalent stops by name as indicated on the music registered for foreign instruments will not always give the best possible imitation of the composer's intent.

Little need be said of the greatness of Franck's music. Even though criticized for the drawn-out passages intended for giving the organist time to manage his instrument and make necessary changes, it is by far greater than any other organ music produced in France for a long period. Much of the music is directly intended for use in the church service or is, at least, useful for that purpose. The writer sees nothing to be gained by cutting measures or making omissions, as suggested by Harvey Grace in his book on Franck's music, even though modern instruments in America or England, in particular, would allow for more efficient shifting from one combination to the next than was possible for Franck on his own instrument.

Widor and Vierne

There are probably not many organists today who would be disturbed by the passing over of such a composer as Alexandre Guilmant (1837-1911), though credit must be given for his significant interest in the editing of much early music that would otherwise not have been available to his contemporaries. The sonatas are little played today, although there are numbers among his works intended for service use that have much value. Even Charles Marie Widor (1845-1937) has taken a back seat to make way for the popular French composers of the present century. As we approach the music of the romantic and modern periods, the instructions left by composers of this period make performance of their music infinitely easier than that of the baroque period where few such instructions were given. Performance of much of the music of Widor must be calculated on an understanding of the ensemble potentialities and procedures of the romantic French school, already noted in our discussion of Franck's music. Many movements of the symphonies have no indication other than the dynamic level desired. From this and the general character of the music you can take your cue for registration. Manuals are carefully indicated, and the basic system of coupling already noted is usually indicated thus:

GPR   —Grand Orgue coupled to Positiv and Récit
PR   —Positiv coupled to Récit
R   —Récit uncoupled
Ped. Solo—Uncoupled pedal stop (s)

In movements of light character, specific color suggestions are generally indicated as well as the specific pitches required in use of reeds and foundation stops.

Louis Vierne (1870-1937), one of a long line of great blind organists, served at Nôtre Dame until his death at the console of the cathedral instrument. His works, although containing many movements and single selections suitable for service use, show a definite turn toward nonliturgical expression. Detailed and varied color instructions appear in the scores, a trend that was to climax in the music of Langlais and Messiaen, the performance of which, without proper registration and indeed in some cases ample reverberation properties in a building will not "come off" properly. Although some of Vierne's more wildly chromatic music has lost favor with performers in our own time, there is a classic and lasting quality about a great bulk of his writings. Strict adherence to this composer's indications for color and pitch are all important for proper realization of the music's greatness.

Langlais and Messiaen

Between Vierne and composers of the present day were many great names: Charles Tournemire (1870-1939), Joseph Jongen (1873-1953, a Belgian), Henri Mulet (1878-1947), Joseph Bonnet (1884-1944, best known for his useful editing of early music), Marcel Dupré (b. 1886), Maurice Duruflé (b. 1902). Gaston Litaize, Jehan Alain, and Jeanne Demessieux have produced first-rate music in the great tradition of their country. Unquestionably, however, it is the music of Olivier Messiaen (b. 1908) and Jean Langlais (b. 1907) that has caught the imagination of American performers. It cannot be stressed too often that you need to take special care in selection of proper registers in this music for correct performance may be the difference between enthusiastic acceptance and obstinate disinterest or even annoyance on the part of the listener. Many passages from Messiaen's work that originally bewilder or stimulate ecstatic emotion will seem logical to you in the end, and cadences will fall upon the ear as being "inevitable," like the final dominant-tonic of the classic era. As an aid to understanding and interpretation of the music of this school we include a dictionary of some tempo marks and registration suggestions that commonly appear in French music.

Accouplé: coupled

Ajoutez: add (stops)

Ajoutez successivement les jeux d'Anches à chaque clavier de façon à arriver graduellement au Grand-Choeur: add successively the reeds to each manual, gradually reaching full organ.

Aussi vite que possible: as fast as possible

Basses douces: gentle or soft bass registers
Bien également: quite even
Boite: (swell) box
Boite mi-ouverte: swell box half-open
Brilliant: quickly, brilliantly

Calme: calm
Claviers accouplés: manuals coupled
Claviers séparés: manuals uncoupled

Decouplez: uncouple whatever manual is indicated

Enlevez: take off, retire
Et: and

Fermé: closed
Fonds: foundation stops
Fonds doux: soft foundation stops

Jeu d'anches: reeds
Joyeux: joyous, merry

Large: broad
Largement: broadly
Le double plus vite: twice as fast
Lent: slow
Les 2 claviers dans le même sonorité: the two manuals in the same
  sonority or resonance
Les deux mains au G. O.: the two hands on the Great manual
Long: lingering

M.D.: (*main droit*) right hand
M.G.: (*main gauche*) left hand
Mais: but
Mouvement du commencement: original tempo

Octaves aigues: superoctaves
Octaves graves: suboctaves
Ôtez: take off
Ouvert (e) : open (usually the swell box)

Peu a peu: little by little
Plus vif: more quickly
Profond: profound

Quelques: some

Retranchez: take off stops

Sans: without
Seul (e) : alone
Solennel: solemn
Souple: flexible
Sur: on (e.g., *Grand orgue sur Pédale*—Gt. to Ped.)

Tirasse (s) : coupler (s)
Tous les Fonds de 8': all the 8' stops
Trés: very

Un peu en dehors: somewhat emphasized

Vif: quick

17

EARLY SPANISH ORGANS

Organs of the Iberian Peninsula may be said to have developed somewhat independently of the general line of tradition on the continent. They lacked the gentle refinement stressed in the Italian school or the broad variety of flue ranks available in the high baroque period in North Germany, and their rich mixtures and reeds make them stand apart in a special way. The tone of these instruments was anything but subtle. Normally containing two manuals, the Great (Grande Organo) and Choir (Cadireta), these instruments were bold in their tonal development. The scaling of Great and Choir was the same, but the Choir was based upon a four-foot foundation against the Great eight-foot foundation.

More specifically, stops were as follows:

Diapasons ranged from 32' (in Pedal) to 1', and included both grave and acute mixtures. The term *"flautado"* is understood to refer to a principal of somewhat broader scale than in use in northern Germany.[1] Listening to their quality in the fine recordings made in Spain by E. Power Biggs tends to confirm this character of the Spanish principal.

Flutes and *mutations* ranged in pitch from 16' to flute mixtures, including the solo cornet. An organ built for the Toledo Cathedral in the time of Cabezón contained a flute céleste 8'.[2]

Reed stops, largely of trumpet character, were available in pitches ranging from 16' to 2'. One special device was employed that is peculiar to Spanish organ design: a set of trumpets directed at the rear of the organ gave an antiphonal effect when used in connection with the trumpets in the case, often placed to sound horizontally into the body of the church. These trumpets *en chamade* were especially favored by Spanish builders. Even mutation reeds were to be found.[3]

The upper manual was the *Grande Organo* and the lower, the *Cadireta*. The character of the pedals was also unique. Some organs had two sets of pedals, a practice followed in Spain until modern times.[4] The second set consisted of wooden "mushrooms," as Biggs describes them. As in the Italian school, the pedals probably served for occasional long tones and did not enter into the playing of parts of a polyphonic composition, a factor that must be taken into consideration in registering the old Spanish music. They also served, doubtless, as a device for the performance of *cantus firmus* melodies.

Particular note must be taken of the reed stops. Brilliant trumpets were sounded by less than three-inch pressure, and the abundance of these stops attests to the great satisfaction their use gave to the early Spanish musicians. Compound stops were also favored. Muset notes that the organ in the Cathedral of Barcelona contained a Cornet of

[1] Germani, *op. cit.*, p. 150.
[2] Geer, *op. cit.*, pp. 238-39.
[3] *Ibid.*
[4] *Ibid.*

nine ranks, a *Lleno* (diapason mixture) of twenty-seven ranks, and a *Nazardo* (flute mixture) of fourteen ranks.[5] Other mixture terminologies include the *Alemana, Cimbalito,* and *Tolosana.*

The division of stops into bass and treble portions gave added flexibility to Spanish organs, and many stops (as in French organs) were only partial stops, for example, the cornet and céleste.[6] Geer notes also that more high ranks were sometimes assigned for the bass portions than treble, and more low ranks for the treble than the bass.[7] The Grande Organo of the Toledo Cathedral organ, built between 1650 and 1700, contained an enclosed section, probably somewhat in the manner of the French Echo organ. This Echo organ contained "a brilliant ensemble of 20 stops, including many ranks of mixtures and numerous reeds."[8]

It is fascinating to note that pipe lengths in Spanish organs were measured in palms instead of feet. Thus a 32' stop was fifty-two *palmos,* a 16' was twenty-six *palmos;* thirteen *palmos* indicated an 8' stop and seven *palmos,* a 4' stop. One of the earliest organs built in Spain of which record has been retained was that constructed by Juan Gaytan in 1549 for the Toledo Cathedral (not to be confused with that mentioned in the preceding paragraph). Since this would be characteristic of the instruments in Cabezón's time, we include it for study. Spanish names with common equivalents are listed, and the three sources from which this material is taken vary only slightly in interpretations. The Pedal consisted of two sets of "keys," each having thirteen notes. Its specifications are as follows:

Teclado principal	first manual
Flautado 16'	principal
Violon 16'	gedeckt
Flautado 8'	
Octava 4'	
Trompeta magna 16'	(treble only)

[5] Joseph Muset (ed.), "Preface," *Early Spanish Organ Music* (New York: G. Schirmer, Inc., 1948).

[6] Geer, *op. cit.,* p. 239.

[7] *Ibid.*

[8] *Ibid.,* p. 279.

Trompeta real 8'
Clarin de Campana 4'
Clarin claro 4'
Clarin brillante 2'

Teclado secundario	second manual
Flautado 16'	principal
Flautado 8'	
Violon 8'	gedeckt
Octava 4'	
Octava tapada 4'	gedeckt
Flute céleste 8' [9]	
Quincena 2'	piccolo
Docena y Quincena	
2 2/3' and 2'	rauschpfeife
Cornet VII-XIII [10]	
Nasardos 5 hil.	broad-scaled mixtures
Nasardos 8 hil.	
Lleno 8 hil.	principal mixture
Trompeta magna 16'	
Trompeta real 8'	
Bajoncillo y Clarin 8', 4'	
Violetas 8' [11]	

Pedaleria Baixo (*Primera tecla*)	first pedalboard
Contras 32'	principals
Contras 16'	
Contras 8'	
Contras en Octava 4'	
Contras 16' [12]	broad-scaled diapason

Pedaleria Agudos (*Segunda tecla*)	second pedalboard
Contras 2'	principals
Contras 1'	

[9] Sumner *op. cit.*, calls this *Querflöte,* p. 355.
[10] *Ibid.* Sumner terms this stop a *Sesquialtera.*
[11] Possibly a short resonator reed. Sumner, *op. cit.*, suggests a krummhorn, and Geer, *op. cit.*, a vox humana.
[12] Geer, *op. cit.*, suggests a wood diapason; Sumner, *op. cit.*, a holzflöte.

Bombarda 16'
Clarines reales 8'   reeds
Clarines 2'

Forms employed by early Spanish composers are limited in number; many employ imitation as a basis of construction. Pedrell notes that in the compositions of Cabezón "are found all the germinal elements of instrumental music that, passing through Frescobaldi, lead eventually to the orchestra of Haydn." [13]

Cabezón was especially noted for his use of the variation form (*diferencias*) in the working out of thematic ideas. The term *glosa* was also used by him for "simple figurative variations of harmonized psalm tones." [14] For a suggested approach to the registration of such variations, we have chosen his "Variations on the Milanese Galliard." By using primarily manual tone coupled to the pedal, you can avoid the mistake of making the pedal stops a real part of the polyphonic ensemble. Do not forget, however, that a rich reed-mixture ensemble could be played by the left hand on a manual contrasted to bright flues for the remainder of the ensemble, and where spacing permits, this technique can prove useful. Begin the variations as follows:

Gt.: principals 8', 4', 2 2/3', 2'
Pos.: 8', 4', 2', zimbel III
Sw.: plein jeu IV, reeds 8' and 4'
Ped.: principal 16', Gt. 8' coupler

Var. 1. Begin on Gr.
Var. 2. At pickup to M. 9, go to Pos.
Var. 3. At pickup to M. 17, return to Gt.
Var. 4. At pickup to M. 27, return to Pos.
Var. 5. In M. 34, go to Gt. (having added fourniture IV), l.h. on the second beat, r.h. on the third beat.
Var. 6. On the pickup to M. 43, add scharf III to Gt. or Pos. to Gt. coupler.
Var. 7. On the pickup to M. 53, go to Sw.

[13] Gilbert Chase, *The Music of Spain* (New York: Dover Publications, Inc., 1959), p. 65.
[14] Willi Apel (ed.), "Glosa," *Harvard Dictionary of Music* (Cambridge: Harvard University Press, 1958).

Var. 8. On the pickup to M. 63, go to full Gt. ensemble with Sw. 8′
and Pos. 8′ to Gt., add 16′ Bombarde to Sw., and combine Ch.
reeds, possibly Gt. reeds.

Tiento

One of the most common "forms" in Spanish music is the *Tiento:*
a strict contrapuntal work comparable to the ricercar. Muset suggests the term may have arisen from compositions improvised or
performed by organists in the process of testing candidates for an
organ post as they were permitted to "try" an organ.[15] A suggested
registration is provided for Menalt's "Tiento on the First Tone."
Needless to say, the enclosed divisions of the organ are to remain
open here. You can begin as follows:

Ch.: geigen 8′, quintaton 8′, koppelflöte 4′, nasard 2 2/3′, spitzflöte 2′
Gt.: principals 8′ to 2′
Sw.: principals 8′ and 4′, plein jeu IV (Ch. to Sw.)
Pos.: 8′, 4′, 2′
Ped.: principals 16′ and 8′ or Gt. 8′ coupler

Begin on Gt.
In M. 19, change to Sw.
In M. 29, go to Pos.
M. 37, return to Sw.
M. 44, on second eighth change to Gt.
M. 55, back to Sw.
M. 59, couple Ch. reeds 8′ and 4′ to Gt.
M. 74, Gt. (16′ to scharf III). Add: 16′ Ch. reed; light Ped. reeds
 16′, 8′ and 4′; Ped. fourniture IV, 10 2/3′.
M. 151, to full Pos.
M. 172, to Sw. (add reeds 8′ and 4′ or Pos. to Sw.)
M. 185, to Gt. (add Pos. to Gt., reeds, Ped. bombardes).

The above suggestions are based on an adequate four-manual instrument. On smaller organs you will have to husband your resources
somewhat, playing the entire work on a small scale. Save what reeds
you have for the sections starting in Ms. 171 and 183 respectively.

[15] *Op. cit.*

Versillo

The Spanish, like the French, followed the custom of writing short pieces called "verses" (Sp. *versillo, verso*) for use in alternation of sections of liturgical offices with parts sung by the choir. It is understood that during the playing of the verses by the organ both clergy and singers could repeat to themselves the texts of the played portions. Organists most often improvised these portions, but some fine examples of such pieces remain. Muset suggests that skilled organists would avail themselves of the short time during sung portions of the mass (sometimes only a few seconds) to change their combinations for the following organ verse.[16]

The Paso

The *paso* is a march-like piece that is played with great spirit and dash. Do not be misled by the half notes (representing beats), but perform them on brilliant combinations at a good tempo.

Other Forms

Several other types of music employing similar techniques to those already discussed are to be encountered. The "Cancion religiosa" by Cabezón illustrates a variety of imitative treatments and canonic statements. Two numbers illustrating use of the block dynamic structure are the "Tiento de quarto tono por E la mi" of Araujo and the "Obra de Octavo Tono Alto" of de Heredia. The second of these works juxtaposes sections in extreme rhythmic and structural contrasts; it is subtitled "Ensalada," meaning "a salad," indicating a mixture of musical ideas. In performing this fascinating work you can proceed as follows:

Ch. (or Solo):	heavy bombarde or trumpet
Gt.:	full to fourniture IV
Sw.:	plein jeu IV, reeds 8' and 4'
Pos.:	full to 1' (add baroque reeds if available)
Ped.:	principal 16', reeds 16' and 8', Gt. 8' coupler

[16] *Ibid.*

94

Begin on Gt.

Change to Pos. at first double bar as follows: M. 24 alto, M. 25 tenor, soprano following in M. 26.

In M. 47 go to Sw. (second beat), and from here throughout this section, alternate Sw. and Gt.

On the second quarter of p. 24 begin new section, remaining on Gt. but withdrawing Ped. reeds. Take triplet figures of soprano (Ms. 93, 95, 97, 99) on loud reed (Ch. or Solo).

Lento, p. 24, remain on Gt. In second measure (103) reduce as follows: Gt. 16′, 8′, and 4′; Ped. 16′, 10 2/3′, and 8′.

M. 118, second beat, go to closed Sw., which gives the impression of antiphonal or echo trumpets. Return to Gt., second beat of M. 130.

Allegretto, M. 145, on second quarter change to Gt., full to fourniture IV; Ped. principals 16′ and 8′, Gt. to Ped. 8′.

In M. 160, second eighth, go to Pos. (full to mixture). Return to Gt., second eighth of M. 166.

On second quarter of M. 177 remain on Gt., adding Sw. reeds 8′ and 4′; Ped. reeds (or Sw. 8′ to Ped.) Sw. to Gt. 8′ and 4′.

At M. 189 go to full Pos., coupled to Ch. reeds 8′ and 4′, then continue alternating with Gt., beginning on last two quarters of M. 190.

Add 16′ reeds as indicated by Bonnet, p. 29, line 2.

The run in the r.h. at the closing cadence can be made more effective thus: take l.h. on Ch. coupled to Sw. and Pos., r.h. on Gt. coupled to all other manuals and containing a heavy reed. It might even prove feasible to add a 16′ coupler to the large reed due to the high register and not uncommon weakening of reeds in this range.

There is little doubt that performance of this early Spanish music with proper registrations is more feasible today on American organs than ever before. And as the music is given its proper sound medium and played with all of the drama put into it by the early masters of Spain, a "new" world of exciting beauty is created for our enjoyment.

18

GERMAN ORGAN MUSIC

The Late Gothic Organ

One of the earliest organs you can study in order to learn the characteristics of instruments before the Renaissance is that built at Halberstadt in 1361. Most noteworthy is the fact that all the stops of a manual acted at once. The specification of this instrument was as follows:

First Descant Manual	Second Descant Manual
Hintersatz, 32 to 56 ranks	Principal

Bass Manual [1]	Pedals
Principal	Principal Hintersatz, 16 to 24 ranks

The *Hintersatz,* being a multi-rank mixture, contained from one to several duplicate ranks at various pitches.[2] Obviously the contrast available was limited, and the spacing of keys, still about one and a half inches apart, made it possible to play only two parts with an occasional pedal note.[3]

The advancement in organ building that resulted from the invention of the slide, allowing for the closing off of any rank of pipes at will, is difficult to overestimate. Variations of tone color and pitch could then be made, and many new and varied stops soon followed, including both narrow- and wide-scaled stops, open and stopped pipes, partially stopped pipes, and many varieties of reed stops, including both the short-resonator reeds (known in Germany as the

---

[1] Praetorius suggests the lowest manual might have been playable by the knees as well as the hands. See Sumner, *op. cit.,* p. 53.

[2] Sumner, *op. cit.,* gives the following ranks for a mixture of the Gothic period: 16', 8' (2 ranks), 5 1/3', 4' (4 ranks), 2 2/3' (5 ranks), 2' (6 ranks), 1 1/3' (6 ranks), 1' (8 ranks), 2/3' (10 ranks). P. 53.

[3] Bedbrook, *op. cit.,* p. 13.

schnarrwerk) and the long resonator reeds. Although it is obvious that the fifteenth century was one of great activity in the development of the organ, and many stops common today were being developed and named, it is difficult and sometimes impossible to pinpoint minutely each stage in that development.

The Renaissance Organ

In his book, *Mirror of Organists and Organ Builders,* published in 1511, Arnold Schlick gave a set of specifications for organ construction indicating the early Renaissance ideal of organ building. None of the sources on this organ consulted by the author agree, but the basic plan was as follows:

Manual	*Pedal*
Prinzipal 8′ (2 ranks, both large and small bore)	Prinzipal 16′
	Oktave 8′
Oktave 4′	Hintersatz
(Oktave 2′) [4]	Posaune (or Trompete) 8′
Gemshorn 4′	
(Gemshorn 2′)	*Rückpositiv*
Zymbel	Prinzipal 4′
Der Hintersatz, 16-18 ranks	Gemshorn 2′
Rauschpfeife (2′ or 2 2/3′)	Hintersatz
Zink	Zimbel
Schalmei	
Hultze glechter (wood flute?)	
(Schwiegelpfeife 2′ or 1′)	
(Regal)	

This information assumes great significance when you realize that Schlick was born about 1460, only one year after Paulus Hofhaimer, the first German composer of note for the organ.[5]

---

[4] Items in parentheses are suggested for large instruments.

[5] Little of Hofhaimer's music survives for our use today. The music of Conrad Paumann's *"Fundamentum Organisandi"* (1452) is scarcely of practical value today, despite its inestimable historical importance. Paumann was born in 1410 and died in 1473.

Schlick's plan included two manuals and pedal with narrow-scaled flues (virtually principal and gemshorn quality only). There is an invariable inclusion of one or two mixtures in each division. Compare the 16-18 rank mixture on his first manual with that of the Halberstadt organ. While there are reeds (Zink, Regal, Schalmei) on one manual, the German preference for reed tone for prominent pedal parts is already seen in the required "Posaune or Trompete" for that division. Although no individual mutation ranks are present, quint-sounding ranks were employed in the Hintersatz and Zymbel. Use was made of tièrce-sounding ranks in the sequialtera and terzian noted in other organs of this period. These were doubtless intended for use in solo combinations.

Early Baroque Organs

A remarkable and sizable instrument was installed in St. Mary's Church, Danzig, in 1585 that contained fifty-five stops on three manuals and pedal. Specification was as follows:[6]

Manual I	*Manual II (Oberwerk)*
Principal 8′	Principal 16′
Hohlflöite 8′	Höhlflöite 16′
Spillpfeiffe 8′	Quintadehna 16′
Octava 4′	Spillpfeiffe 8′
Offenflöit (oder Viol) 4′	Octava 8′
Kleine Blockflöite 4′	Quintadehna 8′
Gemshorn 4′	Offenflöite (oder Viol) 8′
Waldflöit 2′	Spillpfeiffe 4′
Sedecima 1′	Viol 4′
Rauschquint 3′	Sedecima
Nasatt 3′	Rauschquint 3′
Mixtur V	Mixture IV
Zimbel III	Zimbel II
Trommet 8′	Pedal to Oberwerk
Krumbhorn 8′	Gross unter Bass 32′
Zincken 4′	Unter Bass 16′
Schalmayen 4′	Posaunen Bass 16′
	Trommet 8′

[6] Germani, *op. cit.*, p. 80.

Manual III (Brustpositiv)	*Pedal* (side section)
Gedackte Stimm 8′	Flöiten oder Octava 8′
Gedakt 4′	Gedackt 8′
Principal 4′	Quintadehna 4′
Quintadehna 4′	Superoctav 2′
Zimbel II	Nachthorn 4′
Dunceken 2′	Rauschquint 3′
Regal singend 8′	Bauerpfeiffe 2′
Zincken 4′	Mixtur
Bass Drum (!)	Zimbel
Manual Couplers	Cornett
Tremulants for each manual	Trommeten oder Schalmeyen 8′
	Krumbhörner 4′

Analysis of Components

In comparing this specification with that suggested by Schlick about seventy-five years earlier, you will note the inclusion of additional reed voices of both short- and long-resonator categories as well as flutes of varied character (both open and stopped varieties).

Close comparison of the organs will also quickly show that while the Pedal has as its foundation tone a 32′ stop, the Oberwerk has three 16′ stops; the basic pitch of the Rückpositiv can be considered 8′, and the Brustpositiv emphasizes the 4′ pitch. This contrast of basic pitch levels made use of the "unison" coupler in German literature feasible and obviated use of sub or super couplers. Coupling hereby could add another division to any given manual with combination at different basic pitch; however, the Brustpositiv was reserved for separate use for the most part. Although the practice is somewhat analogous to the use of couplers of different pitch in certain organs of other countries, we can only say, alas, that adding the *Swell to Great* 4′ coupler on a somewhat ill-designed and outdated "romantic type" American instrument can scarcely do as much for an ensemble as could be done here by adding, for example, a good Rückpositiv ensemble to one on the Oberwerk!

The meaning or principle is, however, clear. Early German instruments demanded little use of coupling. Fortunately the tradition for a fully developed Pedal division is so well grounded in the art of organ building in Germany that today one finds the finest specimens of great four-manual organs with a single pedal coupler, most often the Rückpositiv (for added melodic possibilities as well as the upper brilliance it can give to the Pedal). More will be said of this shortly.

The independent character of the Pedal organ as developed in north Germany is here seen, as well as in an organ built for the Schlosskirche in Groningen by Halberstadt between 1592 and 1596. Here the Hauptwerk contained nineteen stops, the Rückpositiv fourteen, and the Pedal twenty-six! This organ had a coupler linking Rückpositiv to Hauptwerk, but none to Pedal. The Pedal organ in southern German instruments (where organ building was influenced by Italian methods) showed a considerably lessened development, and this is reflected in the lack of importance given to pedal parts in the music written by composers of those areas.

Resume of Early Baroque

In summary, we can see that early baroque organs in Germany included both principal and wide-scaled choruses, ample mixtures to obtain richness without loss of clarity in ensemble passages, stops allowing for performance of music of gentle character (especially on the Brustwerk, which due to its limited size generally emphasized higher pitches, stopped ranks, and character reeds), a wide range of pitches allowing for variety in solo and ensemble combinations, and reed stops of varied character.

The chorus possibilities of the Brustwerk are also evident, and here we note a wide-scaled gedackt as the fundamental with narrow-scaled stops to be added to it for a bright combination. This method of combining stops is not uncommon in registering early baroque music.

The Pedal organ could be balanced with a variety of manual combinations and still have independent color. On modern organs this kind of independence is sometimes difficult to achieve, for as the weight of an ensemble reaches maximum proportions, the Great to Pedal 8′ coupler is likely to be required. Ample material for solo use of pedals is also present, the highest pitches of these (excluding mixtures with obvious ensemble character) were likely most commonly used for melodic purposes, bringing the pedal melody into position as the soprano voice of a given manual combination.

The Pinnacle of the Baroque

The love of German congregations for their music can be seen in the way in which they gave needed care to preserve old instruments. The organ of St. Jacobi Church in Hamburg is a fine example. Rebuilt by Arp Schnitger in 1689-93, it has been preserved with minimum changes to retain the magnificent tonal principles laid down by that great builder. Bach himself applied for but failed to receive a position in the church. The disposition in Bach's time, listed in families of tone for convenient study, was as follows:

Hauptwerk

Prinzipal 16'	Quintadena 16'	Trompete 16'
Oktave 8'	Spitzflöte 8'	
Oktave 4'	Gedackt 8'	
Oktave 2'	Rohrflöte 4'	
Rauschpfeife II	Flachflöte 2'	
Mixtur VI-VIII		

Rückpositiv

Prinzipal 8'	Gedackt 8'	Dulzian 16'
Oktave 4'	Quintadena 8'	Bärpfeife 8'
Oktave 2'	Blockflöte 4'	Schalmey 4'
Quinte 2 1/3'	Querflöte 4'	
Sesquialtera II	Sifflöte 1 1/3'	
Scharf VI-VIII		

Oberwerk

Prinzipal 8'	Holzflöte 8'	Trompete 8'
Oktave 4'	Rohrflöte 8'	Vox Humana 8'
Oktave 2'	Spitzflöte 4'	Schalmei 4'
Scharf IV-VI	Nasat 2 2/3'	
Cimbel III	Gemshorn 2'	

Brustwerk

Oktave 4'	Holzprinzipal 8'	Dulcian 8'
Sesquialtera II	Rohrflöte 4'	Trechterregal 8'
Scharf IV-VI	Waldflöte 2'	

Pedal

Prinzipal 32′	Sub-bass 16′	Posaune 32′
Oktave 16′	Nachthorn 2′	Posaune 16′
Oktave 8′		Dulcian 16′
Oktave 4′		Trompete 8′
Rauschpfeife III		Trompete 4′
Mixtur VI-VIII		Cornet 2′

You will note the use of mutations. Couplers available were Rück-positiv to Hauptwerk and Oberwerk to Hauptwerk. The devotion to fine organ building exemplified by early congregations has continued to recent times. The metal for the Rückpositiv pipes for a rebuilding job done by Kemper in 1928-30 was secured through tin donations from the congregation.

Today lovely carved heads form the draw-knobs of the console of this organ in St. Jacobi. The writer noted when trying that instrument in 1957 that among the famous personalities represented, including Albert Schweitzer and musicians who previously served this church, were several with horns. These turned out to be the tremulants!

Buxtehude

Due to the profound influence Dietrich Buxtehude (1637-1707) had on Bach's development as a composer, his own organ music and the instruments used for its performance deserve careful attention. Buxtehude's music is great regardless of any relationship to that of Bach. The breadth and importance of the entire North German School, of which Sweelinck has been called the "founder," is worthy of extensive study.

Every music student is familiar with the story of Bach's long walk, during his tenure at Arnstadt (in October of 1705), to Lübeck where the Abendmusiken of Buxtehude had become famous. The fact that Bach's requested four-weeks' leave turned into something like the quarter of a year and the Consistory of his church felt impelled to "call him on the carpet for it" attests to the inspiration he received in Lübeck.

The great organ that stood at the rear of St. Mary's Church (Marienkirche) in Lübeck was a fine example of baroque organ building in the period prior to the pinnacle it reached at the hands of Arp Schnitger, greatest builder of Bach's time in northern Germany. It contained over fifty stops and featured both narrow- and wide-scaled choruses on each of its three manuals. The pedal (beginning with a 32') featured a large chorus of narrow-scaled ranks including a mixture, plus 16', 8', and 2' flutes. Ensemble mixtures (both grave and acute) and solo mixtures were present in all manuals. The following reeds were represented:

Hauptwerk
Trommeten 16' and 8', Zink 8'

Brustwerk
Krummhorn 8', Regal 8'

Rückpositiv
Dulzian 16', Bärpfeife 8', Trichterregal 8', Vox Humana 8'

Pedal
Gross Posaune 32', Posaune 16', Dulzian 16', Trommete 8', Krummhorn 8', Kornett 2'

The small organ in St. Mary's was called the *Totentanz Orgel* (Dance of Death Organ), as it stood in a transept chapel during one of Europe's great plagues; here victims of the scourge were brought. This fine instrument (thirty-eight ranks), like the larger organ, was damaged in World War II, but has been rebuilt and put in fine shape. Its specifications are as follows:

Hauptwerk	Mixtur VI-X
Quintade 16'	Trompete 8'
Prinzipal 8'	
Spitzflöte 8'	*Rückpositiv*
Oktave 4'	Prinzipal 8'
Nasat 2 2/3'	Rohrflöte 8'
Rauschpfeife II	Quintatön 8'

103

Oktave 4′
Rohrflöte 4′
Sesquialter II
Sifflöte 1 1/3′
Scharff VI-VIII
Dulzian 16′
Trechterregal 8′
Rückpositiv to Hauptwerk
Tremulant

Brustwerk

Gedackt 8′
Quintadena 4′
Hohlflöte 2′
Quinte 1 1/3′
Scharff IV

Krummhorn 8′
Schalmey 4′

Pedal

Prinzipal 16′
Subbass 16′
Oktave 8′
Gedackt 8′
Quintadena 4′
Oktave 2′
Nachthorn 1′
Zymbel II
Mixtur IV
Posaune 16′
Trompete 8′
Schalmey 4′
Kornett 2′

The presence of coupler from Rückpositiv to Hauptwerk gave added flexibility. It is noteworthy that no single coupler to Pedal exists, and obviously, due to the size of that division, one was not necessary. The high-pitched ranks in Pedal served well as solo voices for performance of pedal *canti firmi*. In the summer of 1960 the writer was privileged to play the music of Buxtehude on this instrument through the good graces of Walter Kraft, present organist of St. Mary's. That church has a very long reverberation period, and while attending a Sunday *Hauptgottesdienst,* the writer noted that this acoustical feature favored the choral music performed more than that of the organ. Very full organ gave a somewhat muddied sound from this fine instrument, now placed to one side of the chancel, but formed a lovely, enhancing "halo" to the sound of the choir that sang, standing in the rear of the church. Light combinations gave the best results, and Herr Kraft took this well into account in his improvisations during the service.

This distinguished gentleman also pointed out that the *Totentanz Orgel* is, today, still tuned to the old system used in Buxtehude's time in honor of that great forbear. The playing on this instrument of common chords in "good" keys can, indeed, give a solidity of tone whose perfection of sound is enough to send shivers down the spine of the listener. Kraft pointed out that full combinations whose bright pitches did much to erase the ear's objection to keys less perfect than, for example, C, F and G major, were favored by both Buxtehude and Bach in works in such keys as E-flat major and B minor.

Buxtehude's Chorale Preludes

Perhaps the great Dane who, even more than his predecessor, Franz Tunder, made St. Mary's world famous is, as much as anything else, remembered for his fine chorale preludes. The excellent resources of the Rückpositiv of the preceding organ serve well for the performance of the *canti* works. The accompaniment can be rendered either on the broad-scaled flue of the Hauptwerk or with a variety of stops on the Brustwerk. Occasionally it is proper to use only an 8′ register in the Pedal (perhaps the Oktave 8′) or Gedackt 8′ with Quintadena 4′.

The Preludes and Fugues

The preludes and fugues of Buxtehude present several sections, generally containing (*a*) a free, toccata-like section, (*b*) a fugue in duple meter, (*c*) another section of toccata or recitative character, (*d*) a second fugue in triple meter, and (*e*) a brilliant finale. Although he varied this form on occasion, Buxtehude was obviously fond of the five-section arrangement. It is a block dynamic and is best interpreted with registration contrasts to suit the character of each part. No changes are required in the course of a given fugue except, perhaps, where a free close is involved, such as that in the duple fugue of the "Prelude and Fugue in G Minor."

Böhm

Another reconstructed organ the writer played was that at St. John's Church in Lüneburg. Originally built in 1551-53 by Hendrick Niehoff from the Netherlands, it has been rebuilt six times since, the last reconstruction being in 1952-54. At that time it finally received the definitive specifications requested by Georg Böhm but not quite achieved during the reconstruction made in his own lifetime. Specifications follow:

Hauptwerk

Principal 16'
Quintadena 16'
Octave 8'
Gedackt 8'
Octave 4'
Cor de Nuit 4'
Quinte 2 2/3'
Octave 2'
Bauern Flöte 2'
Mixtur VI-VIII
Scharff IV-V
Trompete 16'
Trompete 8'
Schalmey 4'

Rückpositiv

Principal 8'
Quintadena 8'
Holzgedackt 8'
Rohrflöte 4'
Waldflöte 2'
Sifflöte 1 1/3'
Scharff V-VII
Bärpfeife 8'
Dulcian 16'

Couplers

Oberwerk to Hauptwerk
Rückpositiv to Hauptwerk
Rückpositiv to Pedal
Tremulants for Oberwerk and
    Rückpositiv

Oberwerk

Principal 8'
Rohrflöte 8'
Octave 4'
Blockflöte 4'
Nasat 2 2/3'
Gemshorn 2'
Octave 1'
Terzian II
Mixtur V-VI
Zymbel III
Trompete 8'
Dulzian 8'

Pedal

Principal 16'
Subbass 16'
Octave 8'
Gedackt 8'
Octave 4'
Cor de Nuit 2'
Bauernflöte 1'
Rauschpfeife II
Mixtur VIII
Contra Posaune 32'
Posaune 16'
Trompete 8'
Trompete 4'
Cornet 2'

It is interesting to note that Rudolf von Beckerath of Hamburg while reconstructing the "Böhm organ" incorporated mechanical action into it. The sound of this fine instrument in the huge body of

106

St. John's is a thrilling experience indeed, and the music of Böhm makes us wish that this highly talented organ composer had left more works for the organ than he did. Böhm's coloratura treatment doubtless reflects an influence of the fine music at the nearby French Court of Celle.

"The Prelude and Fugue in C Major"

This composition by Böhm would require a good complement of brilliant Pedal stops for its fine opening pedal solo, illustrating well the use made of pedals by the organists of the North German school.

After the pedal solo the chordal passages that follow (beginning in M. 16) require contrasted strong and clear combinations on Hauptwerk (r.h.) and Oberwerk (l.h.). The sustained, lyric passages could be played on a somewhat reduced Hauptwerk, with the fugue entrance beginning on the Oberwerk (M. 35). In M. 47 take the alto subject entrance on the Hauptwerk (plus the tenor, beginning on the last eighth of M. 47), transferring the remaining soprano to Hauptwerk on the fourth eighth of M. 51. In M. 52, starting with soprano on the fourth eighth, you can again go to a secondary manual (Oberwerk or possibly Rückpositiv), returning to Hauptwerk as follows: tenor on the fourth eighth of the measure, adding alto and soprano consecutively in M. 60 (on the sixth and eighth eights respectively). The trompete 8' and mixtur could be added with the first g in M. 63 where the subject returns (dominant). The thirty-second-note runs in the close could be echoed on Rückpositiv and Oberwerk, with the final cadence chords coming again on the Hauptwerk.

Admittedly on American organs, it is often not possible to secure good ensemble combinations on two secondary manuals, but the above furnishes a possible scheme.

Böhm's "Partita"

This piece written on the chorale "Ach wie flüchtig, ach wie nichtig" is a fine example of variation treatment though its counterpoint seems rudimentary at times if we must compare it with even the youthful works in that form by Bach. Possible registration schemes based on Böhm's organ might be something like the following:

Part. 1 (the chorale). Hauptwerk: Principals 8' and 4'.

Part. 2 Rückpositiv: Quintadena 8', Rohrflöte 4'.

Part. 3 L.h., Hauptwerk: Gedackt 8'. R.h., Oberwerk: Rohrflöte 8', Blockflöte 4', Terzian II.

Part. 4 Oberwerk: Rohrflöte 8', Zimbel III.

Part. 5 Hauptwerk: Octave 8', Cor de Nuit 4', Quinte 2 2/3'.

Part. 6 R.h., Rückpositiv: Bärpfeife 8', Rohrflöte 4'.
L.h., Oberwerk: Rohrflöte 8'.

Part. 7 Open on Hauptwerk: Gedackt 8', Octave 4'. After the double bar alternate between the above and this combination— Rückpositiv: Quintadena 8', Sifflöte 1 1/3'.

Part. 8 Begin on Hauptwerk: Principals 8' and 4', Mixtur. At the double bar, change to Oberwerk: Rohrflöte 8', Octave 4', Gemshorn 2', Octave 1'. For the repetition change to Hauptwerk, possibly taking the very last six measures on a quieter Rückpositiv combination: Quintadena 8', Waldflöte 2'.

It would be instructive to continue with various other important organists of Germany. You will note the lack of importance given to pedals in the works of middle and southern German composers in general, reflecting the influence of the Italian school in their scant Pedal divisions. As a result, for example, works of Pachelbel in toccata form show none of the brilliant use of pedals found in the works of Böhm or Buxtehude.

Bach's Organs

It is natural that we are keenly interested in the actual instruments upon which Bach performed or that were at his disposal at various times. We need not assume, however, that he limited himself to writing for these exact organs. Among the earliest instruments he used were those at Arnstadt and Mühlhausen, the latter being by far the larger of the two. The fact that Bach remained at Mühlhausen only one year indicates that he considered numerous factors of greater importance than the disposition of the instrument at his immediate disposal. Bach had a wide technical knowledge of the mechanics of the organ as well as an apparently acute musical judgment of desired tonal qualities. In his dealings with various churches as organist or simply as an individual payed to assess an instrument or determine the extent of needed repairs, he showed great understanding of the task entrusted to him. The fact that he liked special effects could be gathered from his disposition to cherish the use of reeds for special effects. At his disposal were stops like the glockenspiel and the tremulant. Although stops are present whose nomenclatures associate them with the family of string tone, these in Bach's time occupied the least sizable department of any organ in which they were used, and they were of the foundational character of a geigen-prinzipal. Bach had opportunity to hear the diapason céleste (unda maris) but, as far as we know, showed no special interest in the stop. Specifications for the two early organs Bach used follow.

Arnstadt Organ

In Spitta we read of Bach's installation: "He then went through a solemn installation, and received a somewhat sweeping exhortation to 'industry and fidelity to his calling,' and to all that might 'become an honourable servant and organist before God, the worshipful authorities, and his superiors'; and to all this he pledged himself on August 14, 1703, by joining hands." [7] Bach was then eighteen. The Arnstadt instrument was built in 1701 by Johann Friedrich Wender of Mühlhausen.

Oberwerk	Viola da Gamba 8'
Quintaton 16'	Gedackt 8'
Principal 8'	Quint 6' (5 1/3')

[7] Phillipp Spitta, *Johann Sebastian Bach,* trans. Clara Bell and J. A. Fuller-Maitland (New York: Dover Publications, Inc., 1951), I, 223-24.

Octave 4'
Mixture IV
Gemshorn 8'
Cymbel II
Trompete 8'
Cymbelstern
Tremulant

Brustpositiv
Lieblich gedackt 8'
Principal 4'
Spitzflöte 4'

Quint 3' (2/3')
Sesquialtera II
Nachthorn 4'
Mixture II

Pedal
Sub-bass 16'
Octave 8'
Flötenbass 4'
Posaune 16'
Cornet 2'

St. Blasius Organ, Mühlhausen

Bach's tenure in Mühlhausen was in the year 1707-08. Specifications of this organ were as follows:

Oberwerk
Bourdon 16'
Surdun 16'
Principal 8'
Spitzflöte 8'
Salicional 8'
Octave 4'
Offenflöte 4'
Quint 2 2/3'
Superoctave 2'
Waldhorn 2'
Sexte 1 2/3'
Sifflöte 1'
Mixture VI-VIII
Mixture VI
Zink

Brust-positiv
Principal 8'
Gedackt 8'
Quintatön 8'
Hohlflöte 4'
Quintatön 4'
Querflöte 4'

Quint 2 2/3'
Superoctave 2'
Gemshorn 2'
Tertian II
Sifflöte 1'
Mixture VI
Dulcian 16'
Krummhorn 8'

Rückpositiv
Salicional 16'
Principal 8'
Viol-di-gamba 8'
Hohlflöte 8'
Spitzflöte 4'
Flöte douce 4'
Quint 2 2/3'
Waldflöte 2'
Tertian II
Cymbel IV
Harfen-regal 16'
Hautbois 8'
Trompete 4'

110

Pedal

Sub-bass 32'
Principal 16'
Sub-bass 16'
Octave 8'
Waldflöte 8'
Octave 4'
Quintatön 4'
Nachthorn 4'
Superoctave 2'

Super superoctave 1'
Mixture X
Posaune 32'
Posaune 16'
Dulcian 16'
Trompete 8'
Krummhorn 8'
Schalmey 4'
Cornet 2'

Weimar Castle Organ

Many of Bach's fine works were composed at Weimar during his tenure (1708-17). Specifications of the organ were as follows:

Oberwerk

Quintatön 16'
Principal 8'
Gemshorn 8'
Gedackt 8'
Quintatön 4'
Octave 4'
Mixture VI
Cymbel III
Glockenspiel

Brust-Positiv

Principal 8'
Viol-di-gamba 8'
Gedackt 8'
Kleingedackt 4'
Octave 4'
Waldflöte 2'
Sesquialtera
Trompete 8'

Pedal

Gross untersatz 32'
Sub-bass 16'
Violon-bass 16'
Principal-bass 8'
Posaun-bass 16'
Cornet-bass 4'

Leipzig

Two instruments at Bach's disposal in Leipzig were those at the University Church and St. Thomas' Church. Although he was primarily occupied with his cantorial duties, his activity in composing

organ works produced some of the instrument's profoundest literature.

The instrument at the University Church was built by Johann
Scheibe in 1716.[8]

Hauptwerk

Gross Principal 16'
Gross Quintatön 16'
Klein Principal 8'
Flûte Allemande 8'
Gemshorn 8'
Octave 4'
Qint 3' (2 2/3')
Quinta-Nasat 3'
Octavina 2'
Waldflöte 2'
Gross Mixture V-VI
Cornet III
Zink (Cornet?) II

Brustwerk

Grobgedackt 16' [9]
Principal 8'
Viola di Gamba naturelle 8' [10]
Grobgedackt 8'
Octave 4'
Rohrflöte 4'
Octave 2'
Nasat 3'
Sedecima 1'
Schweizerpfeife 1'
Largo (Larigot?)
Mixture III
Helle Cymbel II

Rückpositiv

Lieblich Gedackt 8'
Quintatön 8'
Flûte douce 4'
Quintadecima 4'
Decimanona 3'
Hohlflöte 2'
Viola 2'
Vigesima nona 1'
Weitpfeife 1'
Mixture III
Helle Cymbel II
Sertin (Serpent?) 8'

Pedal

Gross Principal 16'
Gross Quintatön 16'
Octave 8'
Octave 4'
Quint 3'
Mixture V-VI
Jubal 8'
Gross Quint 6' (5 1/3')
Nachthorn 4'
Octave 2'
Principal 16'
Sub-bass 16'
Posaune 16'
Trompete 8'
Hohlflöte 1'
Mixture IV

[8] William H. Barnes, *The Contemporary American Organ* (7th ed.; Glen Rock, N. J.:
J. Fischer & Bro., 1959) , p. 247. Barnes gives the date as 1717.
[9] A. Eaglefield Hull, *Bach's Organ Works* (London: Musical Opinion, 1929) , p. 13.
This stop included only in Hull.
[10] Narrow-mouthed gamba.

Pipes selected from the three basic categories of flues are shown above, along with two hybrids. They are (from top to bottom) FLUTES: nason flute (wood), hohlflöte (wood), bourdon, rohrflöte, koppelflöte, nachthorn; STRING: salicional; HYBRIDS: flauto dolce, spitzflöte; PRINCIPALS: violone, principal.

A variety of flue pipes can be seen on the exposed chests shown here, standing in front of the swell shutters of an enclosed division. The small, elevated Positiv division includes (front to rear) cymbel III, sesquialtera II, larigot 1 1/3′, principal 2′, koppelflöte 4′, and nason flute 8′ (wood). Close examination of the mixtures will show "breaks." Note also the use of stopped and partially stopped ranks.

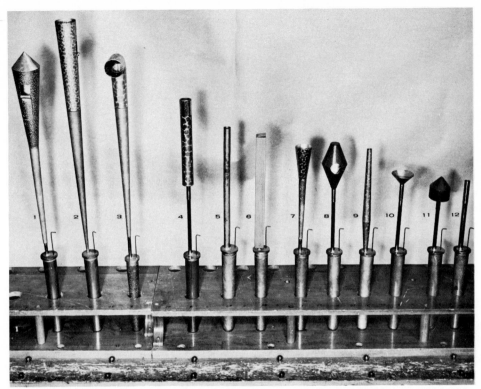

1. Bassoon. 2. Fagotto (bass to oboe or hautbois). 3. Trompette, keen toned with small unison sound and a full harmonic development. 4. Rohrschalmei, useful for solo or ensemble purposes, a pungent but hollow sound. 5. Krummhorn, among the oldest of organ sounds; the clarinet was developed from this voice by fattening the scale. 6. Holzregal, a quiet but penetrating voice. 7. Hautbois, a nonimitative organ stop. 8. Cor Anglais, short length English horn. 9. Musette, stop capable of many shades of tone. 10. Oboe schalmei, miniature oboe or trumpet with great penetration and superior carrying power. 11. Kopfregal, a slightly fuller and less intense version of oboe schalmei. 12. Singendregal, useful by itself or as a bass to other stops.

The reeds in this fine photograph are short resonator types reflecting the influence of the old German schnarrwerk. It is noteworthy that the application of a relatively short resonator to reeds like the trumpet and oboe, stops with normally long resonators, is a comparatively recent development in organ building.

Pictured here is the organ of the Protestant Chapel (installed in 1963) in the Cadet Chapel, United States Air Force Academy, Colorado. This fine installation illustrates an artistic adaptation of the divisions of exposed pipes to the symmetry of the south wall where it is placed. Note the enclosed Swell in the elevated center, above which can be seen the horizontally placed "Trompetas" of the Positiv.

Note the use of Italian and French stop names in the above specifications.

The organ at Thomas-kirche, installed in 1525, was rebuilt by Johann Scheibe in 1721 [11] and twice improved during Bach's tenure in Leipzig, in 1730 and 1747.

Hauptwerk

Principal 16'
Quintatön 16'
Principal 8'
Spielpfeife 8'
Octave 4'
Quint 3'
Superoctave 2'
Sesquialtera II
Mixture VI, VII-X
Vogelgesang (bird song) [12]
Cimbelstern [12]

Brustwerk

Grobgedackt 8'
Principal 4'
Nachthorn 4'
Nasat 3'
Gemshorn 2'
Cymbel II
Sesquialtera II
Regal 8'
Geigenregal 4'

Rückpositiv

Principal 8'
Quintatön 8'
Lieblich Gedackt 8'
Klein Gedackt 4'
Querflöte 4' (Flauto traverso)
Spitzflöte 4'
Violine 2'
Rauschquint II
Mixture IV
Sesquialtera II
Schallflöte 1'
Krummhorn 16' (Cremona)
Trompete 8'

Pedal

Sub-bass 16'
Posaune 16'
Trompete 8'
Schalmei 4'
Cornet 3'

Rules for Performance of the Music of Bach

With some knowledge of the resources of "Bach's organs" you are in a position to approach the varied and complex problems involved in proper registration of the works of this master. A few general rules may be given that will apply to various forms with which you

[11] Sumner, *op. cit.*, gives the year as 1723. P. 316.
[12] *Ibid.* Included only in Sumner's listing. P. 316.

must deal, but as you continue to study it will become increasingly clear that a thorough understanding of the structure of each piece and its spirit and intent—especially in the chorale preludes—is essential to proper performance.

General Suggestions

1. Excessive manual changes or any kind of registration alterations with variety as a *prime* objective are to be avoided.

2. Where alteration of stops coincides with rising or falling dynamic requirements of a given movement, these changes must be made smoothly and without sacrifice of a fluent rhythm. Although it is sometimes argued that Bach virtually *never* made stop changes, we can safely assume that he followed the time-honored system of using assistants for such tasks.

3. Addition or subtraction of stops most naturally coincides with phrasing of the music. Stops may be added on points of rhythmic stress or expressive accent (due to relatively high tones, long tones, syncopations, and the like). For withdrawal of stops a weak beat is normally chosen, if there is no break in a phrase involved. If a change of manuals or registration is highly complicated, there is ample reason to question the artistic justice in such a change.

4. Terraced dynamics figure an important role in some works; contrast is achieved by a change of volume and color involving a change of manuals.

5. The term *Organo Pleno*, translated "full organ," does not mean full organ in the sense that all stops are employed. Originally it meant the full diapason chorus of the Hauptwerk. Some judgment must be employed in securing the desired effect on the instruments of today; it may be desirable to couple another manual, likely Swell or Positiv, to the Great to secure the brillance of the full diapason chorus of Bach's organ. Addition of reeds in the manual, particularly rich bombardes or heavy trumpets, will be found unsatisfactory.

6. Remember that in the organs of Bach's time each manual had a basic pitch of its own, and coupling of Rückpositiv or Oberwerk to Hauptwerk meant the combining of different ensembles of varied pitch and color.

7. Avoid use of stops such as orchestral oboe or flute, clarinet, voix céleste, or broad stops with little harmonic development, such as tibia or dull, tubby-sounding diapasons.

8. For building tonal masses, make use of narrow-scaled stops, reserving flutes or other relatively wide-scaled stops for color contrasts or solo combinations. Reeds of the manual must be employed in ensemble with care if a true baroque effect is to be achieved. If reeds are employed they serve best for chordal passages or moments of climax *where they do not obscure* polyphonic movement of voices. Pedal reeds, particularly the 16′ trombone, serve well to bring out a climactic Pedal entry, provided the tempo is not such as to create an undesirable effect.

9. Employ expression pedals as a last resort, and here avoid any obvious romantic effect by creating the accordion-like crescendo or diminuendo that is called for, for example, in the music of Franck. Gradual opening of the swell box between phrases can substitute for climax not afforded in stops provided on a given instrument, but even here the change in *character* of tone of the ensemble leaves some doubt about the advisability of the expediency.

10. Avoid use of the crescendo pedal.

Chorale Preludes

The first step in registering a Bach chorale prelude is to analyze its form. Melody chorales, whether they have coloratura treatment or not, can be registered in one of two basic ways. Analysis of the music will show whether or not it is *possible* to play the tune on a manual separate from the alto and tenor. If such is the case, several basic things must be kept in mind.

1. Learn the usage for which the chorale was written, and, if possible, read the text to see whether its spirit be one of joy ("In Thee Is Joy"), deep sorrow ("O Man, Bewail Thy Grievous Sin"), rejoicing ("Christ Lay in Bonds of Death"), and so on. A study of Schweitzer's comments regarding the use of musically symbolic motives will be helpful and instructive, regardless of how far you are willing to follow his logic. This method of analysis still provides more help in phrasing and registration than any chordal analysis. It is instructive to study editions of the *Orgelbüchlein* to see how many

115

and varied methods of playing "Christ Lag in Todesbanden" have been recommended over the years. Some would have us play it as if it were a sad dirge, while on the contrary it is a hymn of rejoicing upon the Savior's Resurrection. Needless to say, the music *sounds well* either way, that is, unless we understand the text of which it is meant to be expressive.

2. Select contrasted flues for solo and accompaniment or flues against reed, where proper baroque reeds are available. The length and character of the music will sometimes determine the choice. For example, the great "O Mensch Bewein dein Sunde gross" is long enough that a solo reed might become tiresome, and a cornet seems best suited to the elaborately ornamented melody. Contrasts of color and pitch in the flues serve well for emphasis of the melody. Duplication of pitches, such as two 8′ stops in a given combination, is seldom necessary or advisable.

3. Avoid coupling to Pedal wherever possible.

A second and similar category is that of the *canon chorale*. While the secondary statement *(comes)* must be heard prominently, it should not predominate as strongly as the first or leading voice *(dux)*. Contrast of color is again useful. A good example is the Easter chorale, "Erschienen ist der Herrlich' Tag." The use of bright flues on subordinate voices in the left hand and reeds on soprano and bass statements of the melody produces a fine effect.

The *cantus firmus chorale* is that in which the melody is given out in augmentation. Techniques suggested above will serve well here to bring out the chorale melody.

The *fantasy chorale,* much freer in structure and not involving a direct statement of chorale melody without interruption, will likely require bright voices of the diapason chorus. Note in "A Mighty Fortress" ("Ein Feste Burg ist unser Gott") the fragmentary entries of the subject. Bright contrasting registration on two or three manuals will suit well here.

One or two manuals can be used from the beginning, changing from Hauptwerk to Rückpositiv with both hands at M. 20 and using a relatively soft pedal in the following measure. Hull suggests that Bach at this point used the Sub-bass 32′ on the new Mühlhausen organ, on which he played the piece.[13] Return to Hauptwerk (or Hauptwerk and Rückpositiv) at M. 24, bringing out the phrases of the chorale melody now given to the Pedal by introducing bright reeds or mixture and reed combination. On the last beat of M. 39, change to Oberwerk of the l.h. is indicated, but the chorale which next appears in the soprano should remain on the Hauptwerk. From M. 50 play both hands on the Hauptwerk with ample Pedal but not the previous pedal combination used for melodic emphasis. Do not forget to maintain the upbeat character of the sixteenth-note figures as you phrase this piece.

"Komm, heiliger Geist, Herre Gott" is a simpler case in point. Here Bach has used Pedal throughout for emphasis of the chorale melody in augmentation, and ample reed tone contrasted to bright manual flues will serve well. It would be wise to begin with pedal flues only, introducing reed tone in M. 8 where the melody enters.

Registration of *chorale partitas* would appear in some ways simple, as we are faced with a series of variations, and obviously the general character suggested by the counterpoint of each would determine the contrasting registrational procedures to be employed. Schweitzer suggests that as each variation represents a successive verse of the chorale, Bach attempted to recreate the spirit of some word or phrase of each. Note in "O Gott, du frommer Gott" the indications "piano" and "forte," which call for contrasted dynamic levels on two manuals. Among characteristics which denote the partitas as early works are the little use made of Pedal and the extent to which a small amount of material is developed (for example, Partita II of "O Gott, du frommer Gott"). While Partita III can be played quietly (possibly on 8′ and 4′ stops), Partita IV should be bright and fast, possibly with the left hand part contrasted on a second manual; here we have a "triumphant figure" reflecting the spirit of the text. Although a "joy motive" is used in Partita V, it is worth noting that Bach's concept of joy was often closely associated with a state of mental serenity and confidence rather than with wild jubilation. The remarkable counterpoint of the left hand in Partita VI is supposed to represent a "heavy head." [14]

Judicious use of couplers can help in achieving varied combina-

[13] *Op. cit.,* p. 46.
[14] *Ibid.,* p. 108.

tions. With a super coupler you can secure a 2′ principal from the Swell principal 4′ or a 1′ flute from the piccolo 2′. Likewise if a telling 16′ manual stop of light character is called for, you can use the Great gemshorn 8′ with unison off and the subcoupler. Be careful that you have no note below tenor *c*, in this case, however. In the absence of a larigot, the nasard 2 2/3′ will suffice well, coupled at the octave pitch.

The last category of chorale compositions is that involving fugal writing that may be found in various guises: (*a*) As a *fughetta:* a short fugal essay requiring no change of stops. (*b*) As a *motet:* successive lines of the melody are treated fugally and result in a "series of short fugues." (*c*) As a regular fugue.

Type (*a*) demands only that you respect the character of the music in securing proper registration. Type (*b*) is likely to involve few, if any, changes. An example in the Italian manner is "Durch Adam's Fall ist ganz verderbt." Try for this a moderate manual ensemble with pedal having a light 16′ reed and flues of 8′ and 4′.

An example of fine fugal writing (*c*) is seen in "Wir Glauben all' an einen Gott Schöpfer" from part III of the *Clavierübung.* This requires the resources of the bright Hauptwerk ensemble with contrasted pedal reeds and possibly mixture.

Fugues

From an early stage in organ playing you will be studying fugues and fughettas. The general outline of a fugue is as follows:

1. *Exposition:* the subject is stated in each voice. The second statement will be in the dominant, the third again in tonic, and so on. There may be *redundant* entries, that is, in a four-voice fugue you may find five (or more) statements in the tonic-dominant tonality. Any short connecting or modulatory material is termed a "codetta." There may be regular contrapuntal material repeated against the subject each time (from the second entry on); this is called a "countersubject."

2. *Development* (or "middle division") is reached through a modulatory section called an "episode." Not only does the episode (*a*) serve to modulate to new keys but it (*b*) gives relief from the continuity of subject material.

In this section of the fugue the composer gives reign to his imagination and employs many devices, including the following:

(*a*) *stretto:* overlapping or "canonic" entries of material. Entries which follow each other *successively* as the subject is given out in the exposition are said to be in "periodic" imitation.

(*b*) *inversion:* with subject given out as follows: intervals which ascended in the subject now descend, and vice versa. Inversion may also occur in strettos.

(*c*) *augmentation:* the doubling of time values, or *diminution,* the halving of time values, may also be used;

(*d*) *rhythmic variants* of the subject also occur, although Bach favors such devices in his works for "piano."

The various statements or groups of statements in the development may be separated by "episodes," using the same contrapuntal material as first introduced in the first episode leading into the development, or possibly introduced before that point in the exposition, as codetta material.

3. The *conclusion* is the last section of the fugue, and it is frequently the shortest of the three parts. Tonic and dominant statements occur here, although some theorists occasionally determine the conclusion of particular works to begin with a *subdominant* entry. Climactic techniques often found near the end of a fugue are *pedal point* and the use of *stretto.*

It may be said that the baroque period brought to a high perfection several forms familiar to Bach, those involving variation techniques (the passacaglia and chaconne), the concerto, and the fugue —the latter of which Bach brought to a perfection unequaled in any other country. The fugue is, moreover, the "supreme" instrumental contrapuntal form. It is, like the passacaglia and chaconne, normally a monothematic utterance. The concept of dramatically contrasted thematic units, already suggested in baroque forms but not developed to the degree reached in the classic and romantic periods, belongs to a later period. The true essence of the baroque is the statement and development of a principal idea, like the subject of the fugue. We do find examples of fugues with two subjects, double and triple fugues, and fugues that have a true countersubject, making them examples of works containing "two themes," but the basic idea of the *mono*thematic form is still supreme in instrumental music.

In your study of the short fugues of Bach and his contemporaries and immediate forbears, in particular, you will often note the inspired use made of a limited amount of thematic material. The variety of ways in which a subject can be introduced, the changes in sonority (spacing) you will find, the invariably strong contrasts found in manipulation of materials are raised to a high pinnacle in the music of Bach.

Registration of a fugue is first calculated on the basis of its length and rhythmic character. Short works demand no change of stops for their proper performance, as illustrated by most of the "Eight Little Preludes and Fugues" attributed to Bach.

"Eight Little Preludes and Fugues"

"The D Minor Prelude" of this set is perhaps a notable exception, as it contains a rhythmic structure suggesting the slow-fast-slow organization sometimes encountered in the overture. Here the opening passage can be played in a moderate tempo with a *ff* Great combination. A faster tempo can be assumed in M. 7 with the beginning of the middle section. This can be played on a light but bright combination on a secondary manual, with a return to the first manual in the course of the run beginning in M. 23 (make the manual change on the second sixteenth of M. 24), at the same time retarding to the original tempo.

Another prelude that allows for terraced dynamics due to its sectional character is the "Prelude in F Major." At the first double bar, go over to the second manual, possibly remaining there until the final double bar at which the original fourteen measures return. Some change of registration would be feasible in the middle section —ten measures before the last double bar—where the pedal is reintroduced.

Fugue on a Theme of Corelli

An early fugue of a length that encourages more changes than alternation of manuals affords is the *"Fugue in B Minor"* on a theme of Corelli. Although the youthful quality of the work is manifested in its limited tonality, there is a masterful working out of the subject and the countersubject, which begins exceptionally before the completion of the first subject instead of appearing first *against the answer,* or the second statement of the main subject. An ideal opportunity for change of stops is afforded on a manual momentarily not in use; this device can be used to advantage here.

Begin on a medium combination (possibly only principals 8′ and 4′, Gr.), shifting in the r.h. part, M. 24, last three sixteenth notes (with the l.h. following on the first half note of M. 25) to the secondary manual. Return to the Gr. is indicated on the last quarter of M. 34. The Ped. entry of the countersubject having begun earlier in M. 32 will be somewhat emphasized as the Ped. is still balanced for use with the Gr. rather than with the secondary manual.

Return to the second manual could be made at the end of the Ped. part in M. 62 as follows: l.h. to Gr. on the second eighth, and r.h. on the second eighth of the second beat. In the meantime, however, the brilliance of the secondary manual can have been increased somewhat. This must be done shortly after the return to the Gr. in M. 35, while the r.h. is still completely free.

While the hands are performing the section begun on manual II in M. 62, add to the Ped. and to the Gr. Ped. entry in M. 73 is thus again emphasized, but this time it is the *subject* that is so treated.

Return the l.h. to Manual I, which has also been now increased (a change easily accomplished by the l.h. in M. 74), on the last three eighths of M. 75 with the entrance of the countersubject. The r.h. parts can follow to the Gr. on the last eighth of M. 77.

The last section of the work begins following a strong authentic cadence in M. 90. On the fourth quarter or, in reality, immediately preceding striking of that beat during the natural phrase required by the music, bring the full resources of the Gr. diapason chorus into play, adding sufficiently to Ped. to secure balance. The 16′ trombone could be added on the last Ped. entry of the countersubject in M. 98. It may prove feasible to *substitute* this stop for the 16′ principal; you will have to judge on the basis of the individual instrument what effect is best.

It may be argued that this much change is unnecessary for so short a piece, but the limited tonality and the ease with which the changes can be made, bringing the work to a fine climax, would furnish a fine rebuttal to that argument.

"The Canzona"

An example of Bach's acquaintance with Italian music is seen in his *"Canzona,"* a pair of fine fugues. No great changes would be required in the course of either fugue; certainly no *manual* changes are required by their structures. The first fugue might be played on a very moderate combination, avoiding any brilliance. Not only is the Italian tradition emulated in the incorporation of two movements in contrasted duple and triple meters, but the fugues show a delicate chromaticism reminiscent of Frescobaldi. The second fugue —in which the quarter, representing a beat in the first fugue, becomes a half beat—is considerably livelier in character and lends itself to a sparkling, strong, but not too heavy registration. If any additions are deemed desirable, these must coincide with the natural sectional character of the music. A heavy-handed treatment of this piece would spoil its character, and a registration calculated to make it *sound* "in the Italian tradition" would be entirely in keeping with its style.

Bach and Buxtehude

A careful comparison of the preludes and fugues of Bach with those of Buxtehude will amply illustrate just how fine a teacher Bach found in the great Dane of Lübeck. Bach borrows rhythmic ideas, and often develops them in the same key used by Buxtehude for the same kind of rhythmic development, but his results are always infinitely more perfect contrapuntally. In only one work, the *"Toccata and Fugue in E Major,"* does Bach adopt the sectional character present in the prelude and fugue of Buxtehude. The practice of using one combination throughout a section works well enough here, except that the fugue in duple meter is long and straggly—obviously youthful—and some changes afford relief from its somewhat monotonous structure. The final fugue of this work in triple meter, for all its youthful characteristics, is a joyous and rewarding piece.

Echo Techniques

You will occasionally encounter echo passages in preludes or fugues. The *"Fugue a la Gigue"* with its repetitions is an obvious example. The word "echo" need not be taken too literally. It is better to contrast character and color rather than to caricature fine pieces by, for instance, contrasting four principal ranks on the Great with flutes 8' and 2' on the Choir or Swell. The *"Fugue in D Minor,"* companion to the popular "D Minor Toccata," affords ample opportunity for echo treatment. In fact, the passage work would become wearisome without this obvious structural requirement of contrasted levels of tone.

The great *"Prelude and Fugue in E Flat"* from Part III of the *Clavierübung* illustrates techniques previously mentioned. The prelude is lengthy and of sectional character, demanding a change of manuals. A full combination is indicated for the main sections of the prelude with lighter, contrasting registration for the episodes. Pedal can be lightened here and two different secondary manuals employed, "echoing" the repetitions, alternating between the two secondary manuals. The great fugue with its three sections, built on three subjects, can be treated as follows:

Play the first fugue on a moderate combination of the Gr. (possibly only principals 8' and 4').

Play the second fugue, much more lively in character than the first, on Manual II (beginning on the second quarter of the 6/4 time). In the course of this exposition and development, featuring a return of the subject of the first section with that of the second, add to the Gr., so that when you return to the Gr. for the final division, changing on the fourth eighth of the 12/8 time, you have full Gr. principals and mixtures.

The addition of reed tone to the Ped. will help to bring out Ped. entries, especially emphasizing the return of the first subject again. This is a procedure that must be adopted with care, and it may be well to limit the use of reed tone to the final two entries of the first subject, starting only ten measures from the close.

The C Major Fugue

The genius of Bach is illustrated in the diversity of his fugal accomplishments and the unique way in which he treats each subject,

123

seemingly dealing with it in the only way possible to secure the most fitting results. We encounter special cases where the usual structural or mechanical processes are thrown aside. The more unusual a structural feature is, the more it must be emphasized through proper registration. One example is the fine fugue to the great pastoral "Prelude in C." Bach withholds all Pedal entrances until the work is two-thirds completed, and then he introduces the subject and answer in augmentation. The only two additional entries in the Pedal are in augmentation and are inverted as well. Such dramatic treatment of material must be well prepared, with a return to Manual I, using a bright combination, beginning on the upbeat motive, soprano voice, beat three of M. 47 and using for the Pedal entry a combination containing reed tone. This work is a five-voice fugue.

"The Fantaisie in G Minor"

This work requires the use of a secondary manual for its contrasted second section each time it occurs (Ms. 9 and 25.) Be wary of the dated, romanticised approach to registration of the fine, climactic passage starting in M. 31, second quarter note. Some players add stops on each quarter, bringing the phrase to a smashing climax on the first beat of M. 35; others try to achieve the same effect by "sneaking" on the first manual, one voice at a time. Neither approach is required, as Bach has built his climax into the music. A bright registration must be used on the Great to begin the phrase and possibly sharp mixture added before the third eighth of M. 35. At the beginning of "The Fantaisie," the pedal combination should be reduced before the first beat of M. 3, where the pedal part assumes a secondary role, and a conspicuous tone in the Pedal would mar the fine character of the passage work in the manual.

"The Passacaglia"

It seems fitting to complete our suggestions for study of forms and their relation to registration problems in the music of Bach by discussing the great "Passacaglia," a work for two-manual harpsichord with pedals, or clavicembalo.[15] Bach borrowed the first half

---

[15] Considerable debate has arisen to this point, i.e., that the Passacaglia was definitely written for the two-manual harpsichord with pedals; however, no proof seems weighty enough on either side to make a final and clear decision possible.

of his subject from the French composer, André Raison. Such borrowing was not only common in early times but it was considered a compliment to a composer to make such use of his thematic ideas. One writer remarked that Handel would be jailed if he were living today and borrowed as often and as extensively as he did in the oratorio, *Israel in Egypt.*

At any rate, if Bach considered an instrument of limited range and color such as the clavicembalo suited for performing his "Passacaglia and Fugue," you should reflect before setting up such an exaggerated registration for the work that it would detract from the work's magnificent rhythmic development. Before the days of the character variations where a theme might radically change its basic structure, as from a waltz rhythm to that of a march, composers relied on subtle rhythmic intensification and varied sonorities to achieve climax and interest. Some writers would have us omit Variations 14 and 15 as being suited particularly well for the harpsichord but not so well to the organ.[16] On the contrary, you may find upon studying the rise of rhythmic intensification, which can well be coupled with a dynamic intensification, that Bach realized that in a series of twenty variations he needed to rise to *two* climaxes rather than one single final climax. Contrasts rather than sudden changes of volume serve well in groups of variations that, like the rise of the sea, bring small waves to mighty crests, reach one medium peak in Variations 9 and 10, fall back slightly in Variation 11 mainly due to sonority created by its open structure with ample rests. Variation 12 is rather full; in Variation 14 there is some lowering of dynamic level and still more in Variation 15. Another increase comes in Variation 16, followed by further intensification until a fine climax is reached in Variation 20.

If you have an organ of at least three manuals and moderate resources, performance of the "Passacaglia" is not too complicated, although this work is generally considered the organist's supreme challenge in subtlety of registration techniques, for nowhere must there be striking interruptions of the rhythmic flow. Relaxation of the tempo may occur at cadences between "dynamic sections" but

[16] See Harvey Grace, *The Organ Works of Bach* (London: Novello & Co., Ltd., 1951), p. 93.

not true ritards. The following plan is suggested as a guide, and shows that many changes become relatively simple when they can be made on manuals not in use in order to have the ensembles ready when required.

Theme: Ped.: 16′ and 8′ soft stops.

Var. 1: R.h. Sw. flutes 8′ and 4′, L.h. Ch. flutes 8′ and 2 2/3′.

Var. 2: Change r.h. to Ch., l.h. to Sw.

Var. 3: Sw. both hands, from second eighth note of M. 25, adding one stop if ample pistons are available.

Var. 4: To Gt., second eighth of M. 33. Bourdon 8′, principal 4′ or Positiv 8′, 2′, 2 2/3′. Ped. may need additional tone. Release the low *c*, M. 33, slightly early, in order to change Ped. with piston. Right foot presses piston as left "phrases" and moves from the low *c* up an octave.

Var. 5: To Sw., diapasons 8′, 4′ (2′). Change easily made while playing on Gt., possibly r.h. on downbeat of M. 36. Add 16′ tone to Ped., M. 41.

Var. 6: To Gt. (diapasons 8′ and 4′), l.h. on second sixteenth of M. 49; r.h. following release of *c*, first quarter. Continue to increase Ped. as required for balance.

Var. 7: Gt., adding 2′ in third beat, second sixteenth.

Var. 8: Gt., adding twelfth. Note how in successive variations where a single rhythmic figure carries over, you can change after the accent of the third quarter of the cadence measure, often easier and smoother than changing after the accent of the first quarter (i.e., the second sixteenth of that beat).

Var. 9: Note in M. 73 how the rhythmic figuration changes on the *first* quarter, necessitating any addition on the second sixteenth of that beat. Possibly add Sw. to Gt., 8′ or Sw. to Ped. 8′ if independent stops for balance have been exhausted.

Var. 10: Gt. Add mixture to Sw., possibly light Ped. 16′ reed.

Var. 11: Gt. Add mixture, possibly light Ped. 8′ reed and *light* manual 4′ (e.g., hautbois).

Var. 12: Continue on Gt. Texture change adequate to heighten interest.

Var. 13: Change to Sw. on second sixteenth of beat three, M. 105.

Var. 14: Sw. coupled to increased Pos. combination, or Ch. to Sw.

Var. 15: On third quarter of M. 121, use a lighter combination on Ch., Pos., or Sw., with a not-too-great contrast of level.

Vars. 16 and 17: Gt.

Vars. 18 and 19: Add as resources permit, avoiding heavy reeds in the manual, possibly through coupling Ch. and Pos., adding sharp mixtures. Ped. will have reached full principals and mixture, 16′ trombone. At the discretion of the player, use all 8′ couplers to Ped.

The Romantic Trend

Mendelssohn

Without tracing detailed developments in the period that reached its peak in the music of Mendelssohn, we may note that the tendency to duplicate pitches and mix flues of the broad-scaled categories with the narrower principals had gradually begun during the time of Bach. This was a facing away from the strict and purist approaches normally followed in most early schools of organ registration. The tendency reached its apex in the creation of many organs of somewhat bastard character. Builders were elated with the prospect of having ample wind furnished by various mechanical means, such as motors run by electricity, petrol, or water. Their enthusiasm for developing greater numbers of foundational ranks than previously used and the neglect of high pitches, particularly the mixtures, led to an instrument as far divorced from tradition and tonal logic as can be imagined.

For performance of music of the romantic period today you need not omit bright ranks and mixtures in reaching desired climaxes. But you can feel free to duplicate pitches both through coupling and in combining ranks of any given manual. Tubas, trumpets, and bombardes can be combined with the ensemble. The resulting sounds will have great weight, if somewhat less clarity than a true baroque ensemble.

It may be argued that Mendelssohn's music sounds well when performed according to the principles of the baroque period. This is perhaps true. But the approaches suggested above also serve to give a character more truly reflecting the spirit of the period than does the baroque attitude of registration.

Mechanical Controls and the German Organ

Added flexibility of the German organ gained through placing of occasional divisions under expression, the addition of the *Rollschweller,* or *Walze,* and new voices for color achieved through the imitation of orchestral instruments are all reflected in the music of composers of the period. Today German organs normally have *Tutti* reversible controls and three or four *Freie Kombinazionen,* general pistons that can be preset at the console.

The rollschweller is, as its name describes it, a device in roll shape which the organist can use for adding and retiring stops with his foot. There is sometimes a control marked *Walze ab,* meaning "crescendo off"; the organist can set the rollschweller at any desired point, then cancel it by the use of that control. Then at the moment the desired "crescendo" is to be added, the *Walze ab* is released.

Composers and editors generally note the setting of the free combinations at the beginning of a work, along with a registration marked *Handregister,* that is, stops added manually at the console. Through the use of a *Handregister ab* control, the organist can change to a free combination "piston" without having the manually drawn stops sounding. In effect, this gives the flexibility of an additional piston. A square is used in marking free combinations 3. Komb. ; when that combination is to be released it is crossed out 3. ~~Komb.~~ .

Rheinberger

The most prolific German composer of the period, Joseph Rheinberger (1839-1901), gave dynamic indications that had specific connotations as follows: [17]

ff—full
f—full without mixtures
mf—diapason 8', 8' and 4' stops, or full Man. II
p—soft stops

[17] Geer, *op. cit.,* p. 289.

pp—salicional or other soft stop alone
ppp—softest 8' stop

Brahms

Johannes Brahms (1833-97) left a small but valuable heritage for the organ. The "Eleven Chorale Preludes," Opus 122, were his swan song. A study of editions shows that the composer did not indicate registration for these small pieces, some of which are decidedly romantic and characteristic of the work of this composer (No. 10); others are decidely in the tradition of Bach (No. 5). In the absence of registration suggestions from the composer, the performer can secure the most musical effects by trying to choose stops suited to each individual number. Often extremely simple combinations produce fine results. Since you will likely study these at an early stage of your organ experience, a few suggestions are in order.

No. 11. "O Welt, ich muss dich lassen" lends itself to a straightforward registration. Try the following, used phrase by phrase in this order (I.—Gt.; II.—Ch.; III.—Sw.) :
I. bourdon 8', octave
II. nason 8', nazard
III. rohrflöte 8', gambe 8'
Ped. bourdon 16', principal 8'
If the pedal octave is too heavy, substitute a medium 8' register.

No. 2 sounds well when played using the Gr. and Ch. combinations suggested for No. 11.

No. 9, "Herzlich thut mich verlangen" (first setting), a combination of Gt. principals to 2' is suitable unless the organ is quite large. Similar foundational color can be chosen from Sw. in such a case.

No. 10 is the most "romantic" of all these works. A good Ped. 8' stop is essential; if not available, secure this by coupler from a division not in use in the manual combination. The low spacing of the manual part suggests the use of soft stops with good pitch definition like salicional (plus voix céleste?) , erzähler céleste, gemshorn. You may find a soft flute 4' helpful.

Chorale No. 5 can be performed on a single manual, as Brahms obviously expected it to be played, with fairly soft, combination. You might think twice before employing a céleste, as the running character of the counterpoint is best defined by a registration un-hampered with mistuned ranks or tremulant. For No. 5 the following type scheme is also good: l.h.: Gt. gemshorn 8′, flute 4′; r.h.: (alto only) flutes 8′, 2 2/3′. Play the melody on a Ped. 4′ stop, possibly secured by coupler. A reed or other bright stop of medium weight sounds well.

No. 4, "Herzlich thut mich erfreuen," lends itself well to a sparkling but not too heavy Gt. combination (where the chorale occurs). For the introduction and succeeding interludes, use a bright flute ensemble on the Ch. or Pos. Balance Ped. with Gr., omitting coupler if possible.

No. 8, "Es ist ein' Ros' entsprungen," calls for terraced dynamics, but the gentle character and the very romantic harmonic coloring suggest ensembles of delicate nature, with or without célestes.

Liszt, Reubke, Karg-Elert

The music of Franz Liszt (1811-86) and his pupil Julius Reubke (1834-58) allows the organist a holiday for the use of dramatic devices. Perhaps the last word in romanticism is encountered in the music of Sigfrid Karg-Elert (1877-1933), whose registrations cannot always be secured to the letter on small instruments. You may find it necessary to omit the 16′ (often merely an extension of the Swell flute stop, most useful in its pedal, borrowed capacity) which seldom produces a good effect in such cases. Before you condemn Karg-Elert's taste, translate the German instructions which as often as not will include terms like *sehr discret* (very discreet).

Reger

Max Reger (1873-1916) wrote highly chromatic music but generally followed the Rheinberger tradition of indicating manuals and dynamic levels. Many fine pieces are to be found among the literature of this composer that have enjoyed something of a renaissance among contemporary performers. Although massive, romantic ensembles with ample pitch duplications are often suitable, a more purist approach with lean but rich ensembles often gives the best results in the fast-moving, chromatic works.

Trevor notes that Reger often exaggerated the speed at which his pieces were performed to overcome the German tendency of the time to play too slowly.[18] In this he quotes the fine editor, Hermann Keller. Dynamics in the music cannot be taken objectively but must be considered in relation to context. A full organ will be a *ffff* or *Organo Pleno*.[19] Also you must reserve the softest stops for *ppp* or *pppp*, a *pp* being accordingly only relatively soft. Careful attention must be paid to indications for dynamic increase and decrease, though sometimes these effects are achieved in part by the character of the music. For the proper performance of Reger's music a good three-manual organ is desirable, and the Choir should have telling stops. Except where a dynamic variation indicates use of a division under expression, a Positiv is a good substitute for the Choir.

Reger was not the first or last composer to do much of his writing for the organ while not having an instrument at his disposition. He relied for a great deal of help and advice on his friend Karl Straube, great organist and editor of many German works over the years. Straube was, before going in 1902 to St. Thomas Church in Leipzig, organist at the cathedral in Wesel located in the Rhineland. The organ at the cathedral was built by Wilhelm Sauer who, with Eberhard Friedrich Walcker and Friedrich Ladegast, was one of Germany's leading builders. Franz Herrenschwand gives us the specifications of that instrument (1895-96) during the time Straube was organist there and did much to perform and publicize the music of Reger.[20]

Manual I (25 stops)	Doppelflöte 8'
Prinzipal 16'	Traversflöte 8'
Bordun 16'	Quintaten 8'
Prinzipal 8'	Viola di Gamba 8'
Geigenprinzipal 8'	Gemshorn 8'
Gedackt 8'	Quinte 5 1/3'
Hohlflöte 8'	Oktave 4'

[18] C. H. Trevor, "The Organ Music of Max Reger and Its Performance," *Organ and Choral Aspects and Prospects*, ed. Max Hinrichsen (New York: Hinrichsen 1958), p. 78.

[19] *Ibid.*, p. 79.

[20] "The Organ of Max Reger," *The American Organist* (New York) March, 1961, pp. 13-14.

Rohrflöte 4'
Spitzflöte 4'
Fugara 4'
Oktave 2'
Piccolo 2'
Rauschquinte 2 2/3'
Cornett 8' (3-5 ranks)
Mixtur V
Scharf V
Gross Zimbel III
Trompete 16'
Trompete 8'

Manual II (20 stops)

Geigenprinzipal 16'
Bordun 16'
Salizional 16'
Prinzipal 8'
Crescendo
Couplers
Flute Harmonique 8'
Rohrflöte 8'
Gedackt 8'
Spitzflöte 8'
Salizional 8'
Dolce 8'
Oktave 4'
Flöte 4'
Flauto Dolce 4'
Gemshorn 4'
Rauschquinte 2 2/3'
Cornett IV
Mixtur IV
Fagott 16'
Tuba 8'
Oboe 8'

Manual III

Lieblich Gedackt 16'
Salizional 16'
Prinzipal 8'
Gedackt 8'
Konzertflöte 8'
Schalmei 8'
Dulciana 8'
Aeoline 8'
Voix Céleste 8'
Praestant 4'
Traversflöte 4'
Violine 4'
Flautino 2'
Harmonia Aetheria III
Klarinette 8'
Vox Humana 8'
Tremulant

Pedal (18 stops)

Contrabass 32'
Untersatz 32'
Prinzipal 16'
Subbass 16'
Bassflöte 16'
Violin 16'
Gemshorn 16'
Quintbass 10 2/3'
Oktavbass 8'
Bassflöte 8'
Violoncello 8'
Viola d'Amour 8'
Flöte 4'
Cornett III
Contraposaune 32'
Posaune 16'
Trompete 8'
Clairon 4'

Study of this specification will reveal that while the organ had most of the equipment anticipated on a baroque organ it had also many color stops: mutations, though nothing to compare with some German instruments; both solo and ensemble mixtures; numerous flues with string-type tone (both foundational, like the Geigenprinzipal, and orchestral, like the Violina or Violin); old reeds, such as Schalmei and Vox Humana; and newer ones, as the Klarinette.

There is a céleste on the Swell. Some stops have French nomenclature. We read that Sauer worked in Paris with Cavaillé-Coll and "was influenced by French voicing." Herrenschwand goes on to say that "among the German organ builders of his time he was perhaps the only one realizing the importance of well-voiced reed stops for solo and ensemble use." [21] This throws a real light upon the performance of Reger's works. We know that Cavaillé-Coll's foundational flues were full and his mixtures, though brilliant, did not too much dominate the ensemble.

Twentieth-Century German Organ Music

A renaissance of classic principles is encountered in German organ music of the present time. Builders have returned to traditional ensembles with ample mutations and mixtures employed for color and richness. Some of the high pressure stops have disappeared, and many of the old reeds of the short resonator category have again come into their own. Brilliant manual reeds, including French bombardes, however, are used for the great advantages they offer. This tendency is noted in the Wesel Cathedral instrument.

While French composers of the present time have sought fullest use of the magic of color in organ stops, relying on massive effect at one moment and exceptional color and sonority combinations at another, German contemporaries have developed leaner sonorities, relying more on texture and rhythmic devices than do the French and using all the old inherited contrapuntal know-how of their predecessors. The French have relied on polyharmony, and with the exception of frequent use of fourths in melodic and harmonic con-

[21] *Ibid.*, p. 14.

struction, most French composers of the twentieth century have relied on triadic harmony. The Germans, while writing in contrapuntal style, have turned to dissonant weaving of voices and often to atonal techniques. The whole mood and intent of the two schools is diametrically opposed, and the resulting works, too, must be performed in very contrasted manners.

Hindemith

Paul Hindemith (1895-1963) is credited with a renaissance of German contemporary organ music, but a little investigation will prove that a number of highly skilled and deeply inspired contemporary Germans were at work producing fine organ music before the date of the first Hindemith sonata, which was published in 1937. As Hindemith is undoubtedly the most famous of contemporary German composers, it may be well to examine his works first. The eminent Catharine Crozier told a master class of her performance of the sonatas for Hindemith. He was, she said, not too fussy about details of color—as, indeed, he seldom gives indication even of required pitches—but he became deeply upset at a variation from the tempo markings given in his works. Obviously some composers are more sensitive in this detail than others.

The *Sonate II* is likely the first of the three to be studied by the average student. An instrument of three manuals will greatly simplify performance of the work. You can set up ensembles that contrast in color, pitch, and volume on each. For the first movement, "Lebhaft," you will need to do little except change the Pedal to balance when you go from one manual to another. Probably in response to queries, Hindemith has included in recent printings of his second sonata a comment about the use of the *Walze* and *Jalousienschweller* (crescendo and swell). He suggests that it is up to the taste and judgment of the individual player if he wishes to use these accessories to enrich the tonal combinations and dynamic variations. Certainly, as illustrated on the first page of the "Lebhaft," he must have had the swell pedal in mind, for in the last few measures he indicates a rising dynamic level near the end of the phrase. A plan such as the following may be used:

Begin on the Gt. with *f* volume, principal in character. At middle of M. 8, shift to Sw. with quieter flues (possibly flute 8', principal 4').

The *p* in M. 14 would indicate closing partially the swell box. On the last quarter, l.h. of M. 19, take the l.h. to the Gt., bring the r.h. down on the last quarter of M. 23, following on the downbeat of M. 20 with increased Ped.

On p. 4, line 1, the *mf* marks a return to Sw. Change Ped. for the passage to begin on the second line, M. 2, marked *p*. Here a brighter, thinner Ch. ensemble serves well, with Ped. tone somewhat heavy (bourdon 16' and bass flute 8'). Return to Sw., M. 3, p. 5. Similar devices continue to serve throughout the following phrases, with these possible exceptions:

a) Starting with the last note, p. 7, this passage of exceptional sonority should be performed on a very contrasted combination. Marked *pp*, it sounds less well, for instance, on an unenclosed salicional than on a reed like the hautbois 8', with swell box closed.

(*b*) The passage developed, p. 6, M. 8 through the first beat of M. 27 can be played by using Sw. and Ch. as set at the beginning, with alternation of the two, or a new color arrangement may be sought through use of a general piston, to give solo reed on Sw. and quieter flues on Ch. and on the Gt. (for r.h., M. 21) bourdon 8' or gemshorn 8' and hohlflöte 4'. Return to opening registration is indicated in M. 27. Take the second and third beats of M. 27 on Gt. By coupling Sw. and using the expression pedal, you can get a crescendo (from *mf* to *f*).

"Ruhig bewegt," the second movement, indicates use of the Oberwerk and Hauptwerk, and obviously Hindemith had terraced dynamics in mind. Performance of the "Fugue" is much more complicated. The following scheme might be tried. (Measures are numbered consecutively here throughout the fugue.)

Couple the following at 8': Sw. to Gt.; Sw. to Ch.; Ch. to Gt.; Gt. to Ped.

Use contrasted light ensemble voices on all manuals. Begin on Sw. L.h. enters on Ch., M. 4, r.h. going over to Ch., last eighth of M. 7. M. 21, fourth eighth, go back to Sw. M. 24, fourth eighth, l.h. to Ch.; r.h. to Ch. on last beat of M. 27. M. 31, alto goes to Gt. on fourth eighth, all parts in M. 32. M. 38, use Sw. and Ch. expression pedals to achieve the *mf*. M. 45, add to Gt. M. 55, second quarter, to Ch. (Gt. to Ped. and Ch. to Ped. off). M. 61, r.h. Ch.; l.h. Sw. R.h. to Sw. on fourth eighth of M. 64.

L.h. to Ch., M. 65. Both hands on Sw. from last eighth, M. 68. (Add Ch. to Ped. at rest, M. 68). Both hands go to Ch., M. 73. Open expression pedals wide, M. 78. R.h. to Gt., pickup to M. 83, l.h. follows on downbeat. (Add Gt. to Ped. here on *a*.) Both hands to Ch., pickup to M. 89. Gt. and Ch. to Ped. off. Both hands to Sw., last beat of M. 91 (box half open, closing at cadence chord).

This scheme avoids the danger of highly contrasted qualities on the different manuals which might tend to distract from the continuity of the structure, yet affords delicate contrasts in emphasizing subject entries.

Translation of German terms used by Hindemith in the three sonatas is given below.

Ach, Gott, wem soll ich's klagen: O God, to whom shall I complain?
Alte: old
Bewegt: with motion
Breit: broadly
Eilig: hurrying
Festes Zeitmass: in strict time
Frei: freely
Heiter: gayly
Im Hauptzeitmass: in the main tempo
Immer: always
Im Zeitmass: in time
Langsam: slow
Langsamer: slower
Lebhaft: lively
Mäsig: moderate
Noch: still
Nur: only
Ruhig: quietly
Schnell: fast
Sehr: very
So wünsch ich ihr: I wish for you
Über: over, on
Verbreiten: broaden
Volkslieder: folk songs
Wach auf, mein Hort: awake, my heart

Wenig: a little
Werden: becoming
Ziemlich: rather

Pepping and Ahrens

Two other German contemporary organ composers whose works are especially worthy of study are Ernst Pepping and Joseph Ahrens. Both men have contributed extensively to fine literature for the organ, and significantly most of their works are intended for service use. Pepping occupies the chair of composition, once graced by Hindemith, at the Berlin Hochschule für Musik; he also teaches at the Lutheran institution, Johannis-Stift—Berlin, Spandau—where he resides. Not an organist himself, he proofreads his compositions on a little, somewhat ill-tuned clavichord that stands in the studio of his residence in the Heinrich Schütz Haus. Ahrens, a deeply religious man and a devout Catholic, is perhaps Germany's greatest living organist-composer.

The works of Pepping display great rhythmic drive and a joyous quality not the least lessened by the amazing contrapuntal complexities with which his music abounds. Performance of the music of Pepping requires that the organist understand the German organ and that he study every composition both as to its form and intent (service objectives) before attempting to register the music. While Pepping is not a performer on the organ, the fact could never be detected from a survey of his music, so infinitely appropriate it is to the organ. Suggestions for registration of a few numbers from the works in Volume III of the *Grosses Orgelbuch* follow.

For "Erschienen ist der herrlich Tag" try the following:

Gt.: principals 8' and 4'
Pos.: 8', 4', 2 2/3', 2'
Sw.: principals 8' and 4' (piccolo 2')
Ped.: violone 16', octave 8'

Begin on the Gt. At M. 39 add the fifteenth.
At. M. 43 the r.h. goes over to Pos., followed by the l.h., second beat of M. 49.
At. M. 54 change to Sw.

At. M. 72, r.h. goes to Pos.; l.h. to Gt. in M. 73.

In M. 79, beat 3, r.h. goes to Gt.

Add to Ped. during the rest in M. 91.

Add to Gt. (fourniture and scharf) in M. 94.

The joyous "Wir wollen alle frölich sein" can be played on this combination:

Gt. : principals 8' and 4', gemshorn 8'

Pos.: 8', 4', 1 1/3'

Ped.: violone 16', bass flute 8'

Use the Great for *mf* passages and the Pos. for those marked *mp*.

A possible registration for "Auf, auf, mein Herz, mit Freuden" might be the following:

L.h. on Gt.: bourdon 8' coupled to Ch.: nagard 2 2/3', tièrce 1 3/5'

R.h. on Pos.: rohrschalmei 8' and nachthorn 4'

Ped.: gemshorn 16', quintaton 8'

For "Gelobt sei Gott im höchsten Thron" (Vorspiel) use this combination:

Gt. : principals 8', 4', 2 2/3', 2', gemshorn 8'

Pos.: 8', 4', 2 2/3', 2'

Sw. : flutes 8' and 2'

Ch. : geigenprinzipal 8', spitzflöte 2'

Ped.: principals 16' and 8', nachthorn 2'

At the beginning take passages marked *f* on the Gt. and those marked *mf* on Pos.

In M. 21 (on the second quarter) go to Pos., returning to Gt. in M. 26.

In M. 34 go to Sw., changing Ped. to gemshorn 8' and quintaton 8'

In M. 42, r.h. to Ch., returning to Sw. on the last quarter of M. 43.

Add Sw. to Ped. 8' in M. 46, retiring that coupler after the first quarter of M. 48. L.h., M. 48, on Ch.

Return to Gt., M. 49, changing to original Ped. combination.

Add Gt. mixture IV in M. 53, and Ped. fourniture IV in the rests in M. 56.

Something of the character of Ahrens can be gathered from the statement in the foreword to his *Das Heilige Jahr,* an extensive collection of music for the service. "The ways to God are many, and the renewing and rebirth of piety through the art of the organ is one of them." The outwardly severe nature of some of Ahrens' music gives way to an impression of warmth as one hears the manner in which the composer performs it. Varying in character from relatively consonant early pieces to those constructed in a severe, dissonant contrapuntal texture, as the "Trypticon über B-A-C-H", these works are the product of a master craftsman.

In the foreword to *Das Heilige Jahr* we learn, too, that Ahrens considers the organ of the Salvator-Kirche in Berlin, Schmargendorf ideal for the performance of his music. The specifications are as follows:

Hauptwerk	*Rückpositiv*
Quintatön 16′	Rohrflöte 8′
Principal 8′	Singend Gedackt 4′
Gemshorn 8′ (wide)	Octave 2′
Querflöte 4′	Cymbel III
Spitzflöte 2′	Trompetenregal 8′
Mixtur IV	
	Pedal
Brustwerk	Subbass 16′
Hohlflöte 8′	Quintatön 16′
Salicional 8′	Octavbass 8′
Principal 4′	Gedacktbass 8′
Zartflöte 4′	Choralbass 4′
Quinte 2 2/3′	Flachflöte 2′
Schweizerpfeife 2′	Posaune 16′
Tertian II-III	
Krummhorn 8′	
Tremulant	

Ahrens also specifies that his use of the term *Organo Pleno* refers not to an opaque, romantic ensemble but to a transparent, strong ensemble devoid of 16′ tone. Although most of Ahrens' compositions include registration instructions, he recognizes the variety of instruments at the disposition of performers and says that the performer should not consider the given suggestions an attempt to supress his own creative intentions.

One work the writer studied under Ahrens was his "Choralpartita über 'Lobe den Herren.' " The piece is to be played with warmth and considerable rhythmic freedom. A few suggestions follow that may, along with the composer's printed registrations, aid in securing proper performance.

Var. 1. A straightforward setting of the hymn, this calls for an unhurried performance with clear phrasings.

Var. 2. *Portato,* or slightly detached, execution lends lively quality to this variation, played on flutes 8' and 2'. Note on p. 3, line 2, Ms. 1 and 2, the mordent followed by the grace notes. These are exactly the same, except that the mordent comes on the beat and the grace notes begin *before* the beat.

Var. 3. Same tempo.

Var. 4. Here is the first notable change in tempo, the beat being somewhat faster than preceding variations. The hand carrying the afterbeat figures is played always detached, the other, *legato.* If you lack a 1' stop, secure it by coupling a 2' stop with an intermanual super coupler.

Var. 5. Ahrens shows fondness for both stops demanded here, the Regal 8' and Cymbel. The figure in the l.h. can be lightly detached after the dotted note (followed by two thirty-seconds) wherever it occurs. Do not hurry this one.

Var. 6. Play this variation majestically on a clear ensemble of strong 8' tone with mixtures and reeds. Take care to observe indicated phrasings.

Var. 7. Play this one a bit more slowly, on flutes 8' and 4' with tremulant—Ahrens' own combination.

Var. 8. Quite lively and detached throughout.

Var. 9. Somewhat slower and very freely executed, this can be played on a *f* combination, possibly diapason and mixture, or trumpet 8' and plein jeu III of the Sw.

Var. 10. *Organ Pleno,* brilliant with reeds and mixtures but no 16' tone, suits this variation. Play it somewhat broadly.

Var. 11. Again, play quite freely and slightly detached.

Var. 12. As indicated by phrasing, play in a detached manner, on a bright 8′ and 2′ combination. Only exception to this style of execution would be that all notes shorter than sixteenth must be played legato to maintain a brisk tempo.

Var. 13. Again render *organo Pleno* and slightly detached in r.h., except on the last phrase.

The Organ in the Basilika of Konstanz

In contrast to the relatively small Salvator organ treasured by Ahrens, many instruments built or rebuilt in recent years in Germany show a great variety of stops drawn from various periods in the history of organ design. One of the finest played by the writer is that in the Münster, Konstanz, an instrument rebuilt in 1954-55 by the Johannes Klais Firm of Bonn. The instrument is supplied with three *Freie Kombinationen,* one *Pedalkombination, Jalousiesch-weller* for its fourth manual only, and a *Crescendowalze.* Although from the point of view of the average American player these devices leave something to be desired by way of playing aids in the management of so sizeable an instrument—sixty-three stops, plus two tremulants, and about thirty-two extra ranks included in the mixtures—the quality of the ensemble leaves nothing to be desired. It is magnificent, and the character of the individual stops is outstanding. The summer concerts presented in the Münster yearly under the able direction of the young organist, Konrad Phillip Schuba, would make Konstanz an appealing place to visit on a tour, even if it were not for the beauty of Lake Constance. Specifications of the organ follow.

Manual I

Prinzipal 16′	Terz 3 1/5′
Zinnoktav 8′	Rohrflöte 2′
Holzoktav 8′	Rauschpfeife II-III
Grobgedackt 8′	Mixtur VI-VIII
Gemshorn 8′	Scharff IV
Superoktav 4′	Trompete 16′
Koppelflöte 4′	Trompete 8′

141

Manual II

Quintadena 16'
Prinzipal 8'
Rohrflöte 8'
Lieblich Gedackt 8'
Oktav 4'
Spitzflöte 4'
Nazard 2 2/3'

Manual III

Kupfergedackt 8'
Quintadena 8'
Prinzipal 4'
Blockflöte 4'
Oktav 2'
Waldflöte 2'
Sifflöte 1 1/3'
Sesquialtera II
Scharff IV
Vox Humana 8'
Tremulant
Flachflöte 2'
Oktav 1'
Mixtur IV-VI
Terzcymbel III
Krummhorn 8'
Kopftrompete 4'

Manual IV

Holzflöte 8'
Salicional 8'
Prinzipal 4'
Querflöte 4'
Schwegel 2'
Nonencornett VI
Cymbel IV-VI
Dulcian 16'
Schalmey 8'
Zink 4'
Tremulant

Pedal

Untersatz 32'
Prinzipalbass 16'
Subbass 16'
Zartbass 16'
Quintbass 10 2/3'
Oktavbass 8'
Gedacktbass 8'
Choralbass 4'
Bassflöte 4'
Nachthorn 2'
Hintersatz VI
Oktavcornett II
Bombarde 16'
Posaune 8'
Clarine 4'
Singend Cornett 2'

19

SWEELINCK'S ORGAN—CONTEMPORARY DUTCH ORGAN MUSIC

Sweelinck's Organ

Although foreign influences on Dutch organ building can be seen, and these reflect geographical proximities of France and Germany, the organ of most interest to the serious student will be that played by Jan Pieterszoon Sweelinck (1562-1621), often called founder of the north German school of organists. In general all stops on the larger of the two Oude-Kerk organs and most Dutch organs in general differ from those in Germany only in their spelling.

With very sound reasoning, Geer comes to the conclusion that Sweelinck did *not* have a pedal board like those which became characteristic in northern Germany but only one of limited melodic possibilities (Nachthoorn 2′ and Trompet 8′).[1] The stops of his main manual were strictly that of a principal chorus: Prestant 16′, Octaaf 8′, Mixtuur, and Scherp. The Rugpositief contained a similar chorus based on a prestant 8′, but it also had other flues (flutes and a quintadena) as well as reeds of the schnarrwerk category. There was a Bovenwerk with flues (8′ to 1 1/3′) and two reeds. A Great (Hoofdwerk) to Pedal coupler also existed.[2]

Sweelinck was noted for his echo fantasias and indicated manual change, as did Bach on occasion, by the terms *piano* and *forte*. In performing works obviously intended to be played on a single manual, it is advisable to limit Pedal organ stops, and make extensive use of manual couplers, the choice depending, of course, upon which manual is being used. Reeds should be used for color or for solo melodic lines and seldom should they function as a part of a basic manual buildup.

[1] *Op. cit.*, p. 258.
[2] *Ibid.*, pp. 255-56.

It is interesting to note that the Oude-Kerk organ mentioned previously has undergone rebuilding many times. The form it received as reconstructed by Christian Vater (completed in 1726) is given below as more characteristic of the resources of a Dutch organ today.[3] There were three manuals and pedal, fifty-three stops in all.

Hoofd Manuaal
Praestant 16'
Bourdon 16'
Octaav 8'
Holpyp 8'
Octaav 4'
Fluit 4'
Octaav 2'
Fluit 2'
Quint 6'
Roerquint 3'
Sexquialtra
Mixtuur
Scharp
Trompet 16'

Rugpositief
Praestant 8'
Holpyp 8'
Quintadeena 8'
Octaav 4'
Fluit 4'
Octaav 2'
Woudfluit 2'
Siflet 1 1/2'
Quint 3'
Mixtuur
Scherp
Sexquialtra
Cornet
Fagot 16'
Trompet 8'

Boven Clavier
Praestant 8'
Quintadeena 16'
Baarpyp 8'
Quintadeena 8'
Viola di gamba 8'
Octaav 4'
Gemshoorn 4'
Nazat 3'
Cimbel
Sexquialtra
Trompet 8'
Dulciaan 8'
Voxhumana 8'

Pedaal
Praestant 16'
Subbas 16'
Octaav 8'
Octaav 4'
Nagthoorn 2'
Singhoorn 2'
Roerquint 6'
Mixtuur
Bazuin 16'
Trompet 8'
Trompet 4'

3 Tremulants
1 Ventil
1 Calkantenklok.
1 Coupler (Hoofd Manuaal to Pedaal?)

[3] Lambert Erné, *Disposition der Merkwaardigate Kerk-Orgelen*, door Joachim Hess (Utrecht: J. A. H. Wagenaar, 1945), p. 6.

Contemporary Dutch Organ Music

Little twentieth-century Dutch organ music has been heard in America, except perhaps the works of H. Andriessen (b. 1892) and Flor Peeters. A study of works of various contemporaries reveals a school of organ playing in which registration procedures closely parallel those employed in Germany. If you are familiar with contemporary German methods, you know a great deal about performing Dutch music of the present day. The Dutch school has produced music of diatonic character with occasional surprising contrapuntal dissonances or chordal cacophony.

In the preface to his *Suite in Modo Conjuncto,* Anthon Van der Horst (b. 1899) quotes the unusual mode on which his suite is based, a combination of two tetrachords; *d* serves as the main tonic and *a* flat, as a secondary tonic. The work is a curious mixture of varied tonal styles, combining whole tone effects with modal and dissonant contrapuntal techniques with more orthodox sounds. Dr. Van der Horst uses unusual time signatures, like $2\frac{1}{4}$ and sometimes combines two voices in two different key signatures. Interesting, too, is his statement that he conceived the work for performance on a baroque organ; he goes on to say: "This does not mean that I should not like to play it, or to hear it played, on other types of organs." He cautions that if swell shutters are used, they must not be used for gradual volume changes, but only for the achievement of different tonal levels; that is, they are to be opened or closed at phrase points or between sections of the work. His manual and dynamic indications then are to serve as the sole guide to registration of the music.

The many psalm settings of Cor Kee (b. 1900) reflect an orthodox approach to registration. Indications of special color are occasionally noted, but for the most part he simply denotes manuals, volume, and the pitches of stops required, leaving it to the performer to select specific stops. Presumably where indications like "8', 4' and 2'" are given with a relatively loud dynamic level, the *grondstimmen* (foundation or principal registers) are required. Cor Kee's son, Piet, in his "Partita on Gezang 265" (God is *tegenwoordig*—God is present), is more specific in his indication of stops than his father.

Other Dutch composers whose music merits consideration are Jaap Dragt, Jacob Bijster (b. 1902), H. Monnikendam (b. 1896),

145

Jan Nieland (b. 1903) and Piet Post (b. 1919). The music of Post includes indication for use of swell pedal, and Cor Kee sometimes notes whether a box is to be open or closed in a given passage.

Most of the works of Peeters give familiar Italian or English indications which make them readily accessible, although he often calls for specific registers that must be secured through substitution of somewhat different voices in American organs; for example, a 4′ schalmey in Pedal organ could be approximated by a 4′ hautbois, perhaps through coupling to pedal. It must be stated that the works of Peeters, due to their abundance and the consistency in style, recommend themselves highly to all church organists.

A few Dutch terms commonly encountered are translated below for use in deciphering performance requirements.

apart: separate (manuals)
dicht: closed
en: and
eenige 8′: a single 8′ stop
een: an
Eredienst: worship
ev.-eventualiteit: eventuality (possible or contingent, indicating a substitute procedure or register) as below.
event. op Man. te spelen: Possible to play (a Pedal solo in two parts) on manual with 16′ tone added.
Grondstemmen: foundation registers
helder: clear, bright
meer: more
met: with
op: on
tongwerken: reeds
variaties: variations
vol: full
voor: for
zachte: soft, gentle (G. *zart*)
zonder: without
swellkast: swell box
swellkast o.: swell box open

20

ENGLISH ORGAN MUSIC

The Early Polyphonic Period

The earliest English school of importance, that is, the earliest generally recognized as usable in organ playing today, is the early polyphonic period, producing such composers as William Byrd (1540-1623), John Bull (1563-1628), and Orlando Gibbons (1583-1625). Before their time the master, Thomas Tallis (1510-85) had left a legacy of seventeen keyboard works playable on either organ or virginal.[1] Their character indicates a mixture of sacred—antiphons, hymns, and two offertories—and secular—Fancy, A Point, and Lesson—usages.

The organ known to these men contained two manual divisions and no pedal, and indeed the pedalboard made a quite late appearance in general use in England. We read of a two-manual organ at King's College Chapel, Cambridge, built in 1606 by Robert Dallam.[2] The instrument that Dallam constructed for York Minster (completed in 1634) contained the following resources: [3]

Great Organ

Two diapasons of tynn   8'
One diapason stop of wood 8'
Two principals of tynn   4'
One twelfth to the diapason 2 2/3'
One small principal of tynn 2'
One recorder unison to the
    said Principal   2'
One two-and-twentieth   1'

Chaire Organ

One diapason of wood 8'
One principal of tynn   4'
One flute of wood   4'
One recorder of tynn,
    unison to the voice 8' (or 4')

[1] Denis Stevens (ed.), *Complete Keyboard Works—Thomas Tallis* (London: Peters & Hinrichsen, 1953).
[2] Germani, *op. cit.*, p. 109.
[3] Gordon Phillips (ed.), *Tallis to Wesley, No. 9* (London: Hinrichsen, 1957).

The leading composers of the time often wrote music intended for performance on either organ or virginal, as indicated above, but those entitled "voluntaries" were doubtless for organ; and Gibbons' "A Fancy for a Double Orgaine" clearly shows his knowledge and use of the two-manual organ. It seems regrettable that no more music for organ by these fine composers was left to us; we know that Gibbons was a fine performer on the organ. The deep interest in choral music of the early English schools of composition and the emphasis on extemporization that continued through the time of Purcell undoubtedly contributed to the paucity of organ works suitable for service use.

Not only did the period of Henry VIII with its stormy religious struggles, resulting in the excommunication of Henry by the Pope in 1533, affect the lives of the musicians but in the period following the reign of Elizabeth I, who died in 1603, another struggle ensued —that of the Puritans to gain control—which had even stronger effects on the course of English church music. Elizabeth had protected the composers attached to her service from persecution for their religious beliefs, so long as they occupied themselves with their art and did not get embroiled in political matters.[4]

It is impossible to understand the damage done to the growth of organ and choral music for a time and the destruction of instruments that resulted in almost complete cessation of the art of organ building without reviewing some of the writings of the period, critical of music in the church. We quote from one Mr. Prynne's book published in 1632:

Histrio-mastix, the Player's Schourge of Actor's Tragedie, in which it is pretended to be evidenced, that stage-plays . . . are sinful, heathenish, lewde, ungodly spectacles, and most pernicious corruptions; condemned in all ages as intolerable mischiefs to churches, to republickes, to the manners, minds and soules of men. . . . [And later] . . . The music of the churches is not the noise of men, but a bleating of brute beasts; choristers bellow the tenor as if it were oxen; bark a counterpoint as if it were a

---

[4] C. F. Abdy Williams, *The Story of Organ Music* (London: The Walter Scott Publishing Co., Ltd., 1905), pp. 187-88.

kennel of dogs; roar out a treble as if it were a sort of bulls; and grunt out a bass as if it were a number of hogs.[5]

The Post-Restoration Period

The next period in English musical life might be called the Post-Restoration Period; it included the great genius Henry Purcell (1659-95). Although Purcell's works for organ are scant and some of these subject to question as to their authenticity, they are cherished by contemporary players. Some of the movements from harpsichord suites are equally effective for the organ and make good program material. Father Smith, important builder of the time, installed an organ in Christ Church, Oxford, completed in 1685. Its specifications ran beyond that of the Dallam instrument constructed in 1634, only fifty-one years earlier, and included solo mixtures and trumpet.

Great		*Chaire*	
Open Diapason	8′	Stopped Diapason	8′
Stopped Diapason	8′	Principal	4′
Principal	4′	Flute	4′
Twelfth	2 2/3′	Fifteenth	2′
Fifteenth	2′		
Tièrce	1 3/5′		
Sesquialtera	III		
Cornet (unison, twelfth, fifteenth and seventeenth)	IV		
Trumpet	8′		

It is noteworthy that the compass was about an octave short of present-day American organs and the Cornet was a treble stop, starting at c-sharp.[6]

Since the restoration of the monarchy in 1660, organs had again come into use in the cathedrals. Germani notes that toward the end of the seventeenth century three-manual organs began to appear.[7]

[5] See Theodore M. Finney, *A History of Music* (New York: Harcourt, Brace & Co., 1935), p. 263.

[6] Specification from "Preface," *Henry Purcell—The Organ Works*, ed. Hugh Mclean (London: Novello, 1957).

[7] *Op. cit.*, p. 109.

The third division was an Echo, generally placed in a remote position in a box.

The Early Georgian Period

This period (about 1714-59) brought to the fore such names as William Croft (1678-1727), Maurice Greene (1695-1755), Thomas Roseingrave (1690-1750), William Felton (1714-69), Thomas Arne (1710-78), and William Boyce (1710-79). It was a transitional period when the Age of Reason influenced art, and melodic invention came to the fore. Since Handel lived and worked in England, becoming a citizen in the last quarter century of his life, we include his music here. The period closed with the death of Handel in 1759.

Maurice Greene was a friend of Handel; he published voluntaries for the organ and introduced a style of playing involving performing on a single stop, such as the cornet or vox humana.[8] His voluntaries, composed of a slow movement followed by a fugal one, contained no registration indications, but were naturally for manuals only. Stops on an organ built by Renatus Harris for St. Andrew's, Holborn, an instrument played by Dr. Greene, included the following not previously mentioned:

Gt.: Larigot, Mixture II, Clarion
Ch.: Vox humana, Bassoon

From this we can judge the resources available to the eighteenth-century organist in England. The continued incorporation of mixtures and solo stops can be followed through this period.

The Swell Organ

Around 1712 Abraham Jordan installed the first Swell organ in the instrument at St. Magnus Church, London Bridge. Geer notes that this invention had already been made by José Verdalonga in the organ built for the Toledo Cathedral.[9] At any rate, the device caught the imagination of the English, and while expressive divisions are

[8] Geer, *op. cit.*, p. 280. Williams, *op. cit.*, p. 203.
[9] *Op. cit.*, p. 279.

often still ignored by German builders today, the device has become standard in other countries, namely England, France, and the United States.

The Pedal Organ

In 1710 Father Smith built an organ for St. Paul's, London, that had "some pedals." [10] Organs with pedal pulldowns were actually still being constructed about 1775.[11] Around this time an octave of pedal pipes was added to the Westminster Abbey organ.[12] Geer goes on to say that although in the nineteenth century organs were commonly provided with Pedal divisions it was not until around the middle of the nineteenth century that works by Bach could be played on English instruments due to the deficient complement of pedal stops.[13]

Handel

It was a fortunate and auspicious event in the course of English music that Handel came to reside there in 1712. His work in the field of the oratorio has dominated and directed English choral music to the present day, and the organ concertos are still among the greatest gems in organ literature today despite unusual circumstances. To begin with, Handel wrote these works to be played during intermissions in the oratorios, which were themselves performed as concert works and had no avowed intention for service use. Only a glance at the development of service music and the part played by the organ there prior to the "advent of Handel" upon the English scene suffices to explain both of these facts. Although Handel lost his sight despite three operations to save it, he continued to the year of his death to play his concertos and accompany the oratorios on the organ, to the great pleasure of the audiences.

Some of the works are sketchy, having been done hurriedly, and only the first, the "Concerto in G Minor, Opus 4," according to Dupré, was a completely original work.[14] The remainder were made

[10] Germani, *op. cit.*, p. 109.
[11] Geer, *op. cit.*, p. 280.
[12] *Ibid.*
[13] *Ibid.*
[14] Marcel Dupré (ed.), *G. F. Haendel: Seize Concertos* (Paris: S. Bornemann, 1937), Vols. I, II.

up of original and borrowed ideas—borrowed, we might add, where-ever Handel could find suitable material for his use. At points marked *ad lib,* a cadenza can be improvised by the player.

Most of the difficulty of these works is due to the inclusion in arrangements for organ solo of the parts written for the double bass and cello (in octaves), without which encumbrance the works become exceedingly easier to master for the performer. Dupré notes that the seventh concerto (in *b*-flat) included a part for Pedal, suggesting that it may have been written by Handel for performance in Germany. As we noted above, there *were* English instruments with some kind of Pedal in Handel's time, so this conclusion must remain pure conjecture. In playing solo versions of the concertos it is best to restrict Pedal 16′ stops to a level of tone consistent with that produced by the basses. This will prove feasible if manual levels are properly light in *tutti* passages.

We must consider the characteristic instrument of the Early Georgian Period our guide when studying the means at Handel's disposal. Performance of the concertos with orchestra is obviously the most desirable means of presenting them, although some very fine arrangements for solo performance are available to the per-former today. One final comment about style could be directed toward the phrasing of these pieces. A judicious mixture of legato and staccato techniques gives the most musical result. Some editions —among them are works of English editors—treat the music in an almost entirely *legato* fashion. Dupré is inclined to use more *staccato* at times than seems suited to the organ. It must be admitted that where a detached bowing is indicated for strings a detached phrasing should also be used on the organ in performing solo versions.

Finally, it is difficult to state with authority the number of con-certos written by Handel, as the total listed in various sources is almost invariably different, and the writer has not had access to all of the works. According to Westerby there are twenty-three concertos for organ.[15]

[15] Herbert Westerby, *The Complete Organ Recitalist: International Repertoire Guide* (London: The New Temple Press, n.d.), p. 12.

The Later Georgian Period

The next period in English music (1760-1837) was also transitional, ushering in the classic ideal. Among composers of the period are numbered William Walond (1725-70), John Stanley (1713-86, talented blind organist), Benjamin Cooke (1734-93), Thomas Sanders Dupuis (1733-96), Samuel Wesley (1766-1837). The "Introduction and Allegro" of Walond shows the extent to which the influence of Handel dominated the contemporary English scene. The works of Stanley are, on the other hand, forward looking.

In performing this early English music it is best to omit pedals where feasible. Sometimes a manual to pedal coupler can be used to simplify stretches. Even though his own works can be properly performed without pedals, Samuel Wesley did much to promote interest in the Pedal organ, and through his efforts to make known the great works of Bach, exerted a salutary effect on English music.[16]

The Victorian Period

The Victorian Period brought English organ music up to the turn of the twentieth century and produced such composers as Samuel Sebastian Wesley (1810-76), Henry Thomas Smart (1813-79), William Thomas Best (1826-97), John Stainer (1840-1901, largely remembered for his work in organ pedagogy). The "later generation" of English romanticists included Charles Hubert H. Parry (1848-1918), Charles V. Stanford (1852-1924) and Edward Elgar (1857-1934), men whose organ writings were noteworthy, though only one facet of a broad interest in creative writing. Their organ compositions at least recouped, to a degree, the loss of quality that existed between their works and those of John Stanley and Samuel Wesley, written about a century earlier.

Twentieth-Century Organ Music

It is to the credit of English organ composers of the present century that they have produced a quantity of what might be called "honest"

[16] Geer, *op. cit.*, p. 293.

music; much of this music, though not of the highest caliber, is still of acceptable quality. A large part of it is suitable for service use. Perhaps the name that stands out most is that of Herbert Howells (b. 1892), a composer whose work places him uniquely high among his contemporaries. With the knowledge that the English organ has followed much the same pattern of development as that in America, with a few notable exceptions, the organist has considerable freedom of registration; Howells is content to indicate manuals and sometimes pitches he requires. It is then up to the player to use good judgment in the selection of suitable timbres.

The two sets of psalm preludes by Howells furnish the organist really first-rate service music. Their breathless rhythms and irregular meters are two of Howells' most telling style characteristics. It is just these breathless phrases, sometimes pressing on without complete interruption in all voices for over twenty measures, that demand a rhythmic clarity and registrational sensitivity of high caliber from the performer. A few general suggestions may prove helpful.

Let us consider Psalm Prelude I (Second Set), "Out of the depths we cry unto thee, O Lord."

Try the opening page on the Sw. with strings and céleste, bringing out the opening Ped. entry on a soft Ped. 8' stop, coupled to Sw. On p. 2, go over to the Ch. coupled to Sw., using unda maris or gentle flues, like gemshorn or erzähler. At the double bar, p. 2, line 2, a dramatic change to basic flues of gentle character (minus célestes) will give relief from the orchestral string effect. Follow manual indications carefully.[17] On p. 3, at the pickup to the last measure, line 2, add substantially to the ensemble of all manuals, closing boxes to maintain the required pp. Additional stops are needed to get the varied dynamics required through use of the expression pedals as indicated. On line 2 of p. 4, M. 3, change to Gt. (plus Sw.), adding light reeds and mixture of the Sw. (or Ch.). Full Sw. is added as indicated, line 1 on p. 5. Although no manual change is indicated at the bottom of p. 5, full organ can be used, playing on the Gr., reductions being made on p. 6 at the following points: (a) on the last eighth of M. 2; (b) on the third eighth of M. 3;

---

[17] Remember that manuals are numbered as follows on the English organ: I. Choir, II. Great, III. Swell, IV. Solo.

(c) on the third eighth of M. 5, and again (d) at the end of M. 6. By the third line all reeds and mixtures will be retired. The numerous accents called for on p. 6 must be agogic in nature. After return to reduced Sw. in M. 10, p. 6, reduce to a very light flue combination at the end of M. 2, p. 7. On line 2, p. 7, lightest flue (s) of the Ch. are needed. Try coupling Sw. (as indicated) with the céleste used at the beginning of the composition. The last few measures can be played on Sw., voix céleste alone.

Notice that nowhere in this piece are Choir and Great coupled. The English organ has retained a substantial Choir ensemble, and this type coupling is considered unnecessary; in some American organs, for massive ensembles, exception must be made to this procedure.

Psalm Prelude III (Second Set) illustrates additional English techniques.

Note the beginning on the Gt., marked *ff*. On p. 4, line 2, note the indication for full Sw. for the accompaniment with tuba on the melody. The English Solo division suffices here, as its large reed will usually stand alone against full organ. Again, on an American instrument, you may need to play this melody on the Gr. trumpet, coupled to Sw. Failing a Gt. trumpet, use a combination of Ch. (*ff*) and perhaps Gr. (8' and 4') for the sustained chords in the l.h. part, with Sw. reeds and mixture on the melody. The interesting Ped. melody beginning at the bottom of p. 4 can be set off well by a light Ped. reed.

Reduce the ensemble in the M. 2, top of p. 5, going to a reduced Ch. on the second quarter of M. 5 with a strongly contrasted foundational ensemble. For the section beginning on line 3, p. 5, try an ensemble of stringy character, the harmonics of which will help preserve clarity in the low melodies in bass and tenor registers. To that you may add some 4' flute or light diapason tone.

Beginning on the top of p. 6, use a somewhat heavy pedal (bourdon 16' and violone 16') to secure the *"poco pesante"* required. On the melodic passages beginning on the last measure of line 3, p. 6, although the indication is to play entirely on the Ch.-Sw. combination, it is effective to contrast flues of another manual, and shifting from one manual to another is easy, as the melody shifts. The opaque texture with its unusual spacing of ninth chords, has a tendency to detract from the unisons involved between the melody and its accompaniment. On M. 1, p. 7, change to a more normal color for a striking contrast, reaching a fairly full combination at the beginning of line 3, p. 7. Add reeds and mixtures at the beginning of p. 8, with ample Ped. reed tone.

Contrast is needed after the climax on p. 9, and a reduction to flues (and light mixture?) in M. 12, p. 9, is helpful. Contrast through indicated manual changes on p. 10 is essential. Reeds and mixtures are again predominating in color, M. 14, p. 11. Careful addition of stops to the end, plus the increasing acceleration of the rhythmic drive keep this lengthy coda from being a denouement. Note the tuba against full Sw. on the third line of p. 13.

Basic to the successful performance of this piece are two requirements: (a) a strong rhythmic drive and careful use of agogic accents, plus good phrasing, (b) the selection of combinations that will properly secure the climaxes written into the music. Too much force too soon, especially on small organs, will detract from the dynamic picture made by this fine work, which amply expresses the scripture set forth in its title: "Sing unto him a new song; play skillfully with a loud noise."

21

CONTEMPORARY AMERICAN ORGAN MUSIC

The writer will long recall a question posed by leading German organist-composer Joseph Ahrens. In a discussion in which he suggested to the eminent musician that he wished upon return to the United States to send Ahrens some music by American composers for the organ, Ahrens asked, *"Ja. Gibt es das den?"* (Is there really such a thing?)

There is, indeed, fine American organ music written in the twentieth century. Because of its unique registrational demands, the music of three Americans will be mentioned here. Their output is essentially romantic in character and makes use of the complete resources of the organ as it is known in this country today.

Eric DeLamarter

The works of DeLamarter show a flair for color in registration. They call for the use of such devices as the crescendo pedal, now considered "beyond the pale" by many young players, as indeed it should be in the performance of much organ music, and take full advantage of the organ's mechanical devices. Such directions as "strings," "celesta or fl. 8′ and piccolo 2′," "English horn," "vox humana," "orchestral oboe," "clarinet," "French horn," "voix céleste," and "chimes" all show a tendency to exploit the romantic possibilities of the orchestral organ. The ensemble to be found in DeLamarter's music relies on the resources of the American organ with many 8′ stops, ample solo and ensemble reeds, and not too much upper work. Careful analysis of works such as the "Festival Prelude in Honor of Saint Louis, King of France" shows that he does not hesitate to draw solo reeds such as clarinet (Choir) and flugel horn (Solo) and bring these into the ensemble by putting on full crescendo pedal. This does not suggest that you must follow that procedure entirely. Where mixtures are available, they can well be used in sparkling ensembles, but with ample ensemble reeds there would be no loss in omitting *solo* reeds from the ensemble. It must be remembered, too, that the Chicago Fourth Presbyterian Church organ contained no general pistons, and the crescendo pedal for quick change from full Great ensemble to, for instance, a light flute 8′ on the Great, was doubtless a matter of expediency.

Perhaps DeLamarter's finest work is his "A Gothic Prelude," published in 1937. There are sections, such as pages 7 and 8, that remind one of the work of Franck, and the style is not too far removed from that of the French master at times. There is, however, a quality of rhythmic freedom, a sometimes quixotic shifting of moods, and radical registration changes that mark the work as typically American.

Leo Sowerby

The help DeLamarter gave to Sowerby (b. 1895) was doubtless an encouragement to the young composer, then almost 22, when De-Lamarter conducted the Chicago Symphony, on January, 1917, in a performance of works by Sowerby. No better description could be given of Sowerby's American characteristics than those words written by Tuthill in 1938 when he remarked that Sowerby's melodies often have a

rhythmic verve and snap. . . . The tunes have a lilt and syncopation that make them akin to folk or popular music and have a quality that definitely marks them as American. This is not from any copying of the negro or any other type of American folk-music, but rather from the absorption of their essential spirit and its reissue from the composer's creative imagination in his own characteristic manner, a process that makes them truly national in spirit. There is in these tunes a rhythmic crispness, a simplicity of tonality and a frankness and directness that belong to our native soil.[1]

It seems significant that in quiet movements Sowerby is more explicit about color requirements for registration than in those where there is a typical rhythmic drive and a moving tempo. A good example of these facets of registration requirements can be seen in contrasting, for example, the instructions for performance of the "Toccata" (1941) and the slow movement of the "Sonatina" (1947).

To say that Sowerby's music has become less romantic in recent years would be, at least to a degree, misleading. It is true that such early works as the "Symphony in G Major," "Requiescat in Pace," and "Comes Autumn Time" exhibit an unusual flair for use of romantic organ registrations, but late works make frequent use of special color, for example, the "Holiday Trumpets" has reed color contrasted to foundation tone; "Jubilee," reeds against flues; "Pre-

[1] Burnet C. Tuthill, "Leo Sowerby," *The Musical Quarterly* (New York), July, 1938, pp. 252-53.

lude on 'Charterhouse,' " gemshorn céleste coupled to light flues; "Prelude on 'Capel,' " soft reed 8′, piccolo 2′, and mixture, string 8′; and so on. Whereas in late works there is elimination of specific color requirements more frequently than in early works (replaced by indications for manual and dynamic level, leaving final choices up to the organist) , we find ample examples of the same procedure in early works as well. It seems fair to say that with a supreme knowledge and command of his instrument, this composer has pursued his creative works in a highly systematic and consistent fashion, perhaps discovering more frequent uses for modalism and diatonic dissonance in recent works and, on occasion, displaying less tendency to be overly chromatic than in some early works.

Sowerby feels that his music is suited for both church and concert use. When he made this statement, the writer with some hesitation asked him, "How about 'Comes Autumn Time'?" After a slight hesitation the answer came, "Well, perhaps for a postlude." Sowerby also admits that his "metronome has been known to be wrong." In other words, too stiff an adherence to such indications might result at times in a performance not entirely musical; the player must take into consideration his instrument and the acoustics of a building and apply good judgment in deciding the cases where a slight deviation from the printed tempo seems advisable. The writer encountered such a 'problem in a performance of the "Ballade" for English horn and organ. After concentrating on getting the tempi controlled, he met—two days before the performance—Laurence Thorstenberg, member of the Chicago Symphony who was to play the English horn part. Mr. Thorstenberg in two different sections, suggested definite tempo changes which, he said, Sowerby had had him make in a previous rehearsal of the work with another organist. The results, *with* altered tempi, proved pleasing to the composer.

A last suggestion can be given to the performer of Sowerby's music; study the specifications of the Austin organ at St. James Cathedral, and compare its resources to your own. The specifications are included for this purpose, and it only remains to note that though the Transept organ was added during Sowerby's long tenure at St. James, most of his music was written for the instrument prior to that "rebuilding" in the mid-1950s. Sowerby notes, however, that he

159

sometimes calls for stops not found on the St. James organ. It is safe to assume that particularly in the department of upper work, the organist can feel free to extend his resources beyond those listed below, always keeping in mind that the ensemble should be full-bodied, when loud, and not the transparent ensemble characteristic of baroque music. Here again, you must make judgments on the basis of the character of each individual work. At the risk of being redundant, the author wishes to emphasize the reason for inclusion of this specification. It will give the student a knowledge of a "vanishing breed" of instruments, the romantic organ. Any organist interested in trying to recapture in his performance the original flavor in Sowerby's music can profit by an understanding of the organ at St. James Cathedral.

Great
Double Diapason 16'
Principal Diapason 8'
Spitz Flute 8'
Doppel Flute 8'
Gemshorn 8'
Gemshorn Céleste 8'
Octave 4'
Harmonic Flute 4'
Trumpet 8'

Transept Great
Principal 8'
Gedeckt 8' (Sw)
Salicional 8' (Sw)
Octave 4'
Spitzflöte 4' (Sw)
Mixture III
Chimes

Swell
Bourdon 16'
Open Diapason 8'
Stopped Diapason 8'
Viole d'Orchestre 8'
Echo Salicional 8'
Voix Céleste 8'
Flauto Traverso 4'
Piccolo 2'
Dolce Cornet III
Contra Fagotto 16'
Cornopean 8'
Oboe 8'
Vox Humana 8'
Tremulant

Transept Swell
Gedeckt 8'
Salicional 8'
Voix Céleste 8'
Flauto Dolce 8'
Spitzflöte 4'
Blockflöte 2'
Trumpet 8'
Tremulant

Choir

Open Diapason 8'
Concert Flute 8'
Unda Maris 8'
Dulciana 8'
Flûte d'Amour 4'
Flautino 2'
Clarinet 8'
Tremulant

Solo

Flauto Major 8'
Stentorphone 8'
Gross Gamba 8'
Gamba Céleste 8'
Flûte Ouverte 4'
Tuba Profunda 16'
Harmonic Tuba 8'
Harmonic Clarion 4'
Cor Anglais 8'
Tremulant
Chimes

Pedal

Resultant Bass 32'
Open Diapason 16'
Violone 16'
Bourdon 16'
Second Bourdon 16' (Sw)
Gross Flute 8' (Solo)
Tuba Profunda 16' (Solo)
Contra Fagotto 16' (Sw)
Harmonic Tuba 8' (Solo)

Transept Pedal

Bourdon 16'
Gedeckt 16'
Principal 8'
Gedeckt 8' (Sw)
Choral Bass 4'

Seth Bingham

This composer (b. 1882), like DeLamarter, studied with Widor and Guilmant. As a professor at Columbia University and lecturer at Union Theological Seminary in New York City, Bingham has exerted considerable influence on American church music and organ literature in particular. The writer has heard no finer music for organ and orchestra than the "Connecticut Suite" performed in 1957 in Westminster Abbey by the eminent American organist, Marilyn Mason. Many of the characteristics that mark the music of DeLamarter and Sowerby as American can be found in the works of Bingham. They possess a spirited rhythmic sense and require an intimate control of the instrument and a knowing use of orchestral effects. A work of late date, published in 1959, is the "Sonata of Prayer and Praise." The first movement, "Prelude to Worship," reveals a mastery of form and registration detail not often surpassed in twentieth-century organ literature in any country. You can understand how difficult it would be to perform this piece on a European organ with its few general pistons; numerous generals, individual manual pistons, the crescendo pedal, manual to pedal reversible, and on top of that, some hand registration are needed to bring the work to a successful performance. Indeed, it is a fine and rewarding study for the young organist (as well as any other) who would perfect his command of his instrument in the handling of romantic music.

22

HYMN ACCOMPANIMENTS

Hymn playing is one of the most important jobs the organist must learn. In addition to the all-important problems of setting and maintaining proper singing tempos for hymns of varying character, playing good introductions, good phrasing, and proper executing of repeated notes, there is the major issue of good choice of registration.

The Element of Variety

To begin with, you must know each hymn well enough to select registrations that will carefully carry out the general spirit and sense of the text. The size of the organ at your disposal may create problems in variety. Assuming that you have an adequate instrument, we suggest that although it is not necessary to make continuous registration changes in the course of a hymn, some changes can be useful in underlining the meaning of the text. Take for example "The King of Love My Shepherd Is" (*Dominus Regit Me*) by Dykes. This fine text based on the twenty-third psalm presents a buildup of poetic fervor through the third line:

> Perverse and foolish oft I strayed,
> But yet in love he sought me,
> And on his shoulder gently laid,
> And home, rejoicing, brought me.

A rather bright registration used up to this point could be followed by something more subdued on the fourth stanza which begins "In death's dark vale. . . ." Buildup of tone could follow on stanza five, and the sixth could be a really brilliant accompaniment with reeds and mixtures:

> And so through all the length of days
> Thy goodness faileth never:
> Good Shepherd, may I sing thy praise
> Within thy house forever.

A few words of caution may be helpful. The organist should never frighten the members of the congregation by too great a drop of dynamic level, thereby leaving them with the feeling of lack of support and discouraging participation.

The Unaccompanied Stanza

While it is not only possible but a very excellent idea to sing an occasional hymn stanza entirely unaccompanied, this must be done with care. It is inadvisable to try this on a day when your congregation looks uncomfortably small. To start with you need a familiar hymn, and you should employ unaccompanied singing only where it seems suitable to the text. Use your choir as a firm guide for the congregation.

Play the first chord of the stanza somewhat lightly as if you intended to accompany it and then drop out completely, leaving the choir to lead. On the very last chord you can subtly come in under the singing, holding out the chord for the normal length, phrasing, and reentering as if you had been playing all along. When a congregation is accustomed to this occasional technique, they enjoy it and always participate with added pleasure. Do not forget the important features: (*a*) Begin and end with organ; (*b*) keep the choir going on a good steady tempo; and (*c*) use the technique where it has meaning and not merely as a device for variety. Needless to say, variety as an end in itself is not a very worthy goal.

Hymns of Praise; Solo Style

Hymns of praise must have bright ensemble accompaniments, utilizing diapason choruses with mixtures, varying by use of reeds. If the Great reed is too large for normal congregational use (except when the church is filled on holidays!), you may find it useful for accompaniment of a unison stanza, possibly third or last stanza of a four-stanza hymn. In such cases Choir and Swell coupled—with flue choruses, mixtures, and reeds—make a good foil for the full Great with bombarde or trumpet added on the melody. Do not forget to retire the Great to Pedal coupler when using this type registration!

It is not beyond reason to use a fine Pedal organ with reeds and mixtures for a unison melody, reharmonizing and playing the accompaniment on a clear manual combination—possibly using only Great diapason chorus with acute mixtures or Swell with foundation tone, mixtures, and reeds. This is not a device for beginners, and had better be avoided unless it can be done successfully. A bulletin note to the congregation that unison singing with free accompaniment is expected for a certain stanza can save a good deal of confusion and uncertainty.

Another good device for varying bright accompaniments is to play one stanza on Swell reeds and mixtures, answering it by the full flues and mixtures on the Great (and Choir). Here of course, a sizeable organ is presumed.

Quiet Hymns

Accompaniment for hymns of prayer, consecration, and petition call for less organ than praise and thanksgiving hymns. Accompaniments that are light and bright, minus heavy unison flues and reeds, are generally effective. You must at all times guard against "underplaying" the congregation. Leadership from the console is essential, and slightly overplaying is safer than underplaying for average circumstances. Even in this type hymn, variety can be gained from playing the soprano in solo style (as suggested previously) where unison singing is employed on a certain stanza; it will only be necessary to lower the level of both the accompaniment and the solo manual—possibly using full Great flues, except for acute mixtures, against Swell and Choir flues.

A hymn of preparation for communion may sound well when played with foundation tone (8′ and 4′ stops only). Unless the congregation is one that generally sings well and does not drag, this practice is dangerous as it gives minimum support for singing.

An occasional stanza without Pedal can be a great relief.

Sound advice for good performance of hymn accompaniments might be summed up briefly by saying: (a) Know your hymns well as to notes and texts; (b) make the tempo and registration suit the text, as well as the basic rhythmic character of the music; and (c) play with confidence and give the support that makes for confident singing.

If you find that you are continually fighting your congregation on hymns, several things can be wrong. You may have difficult accoustical problems that create a lag in the sound that reaches you from the body of the church. It may be then that only by playing slightly *ahead* of the congregation can you actually be playing *with* them and not dragging. Your choice of tempo or registration may be faulty; good organ accompanying does not "interfere" with comfortable singing. It must not drag or race uncomfortably; it should of all things not vary from one stanza to another. If your congregation has singing potential but you get poor results, it may be that you need some educational program with the help of the minister to stimulate

165

activity and insure successful participation of the congregation.[1] A choral vesper devoted to hymns and congregational participation can do much to engender enthusiasm.

23

VOCAL AND CHORAL ACCOMPANIMENTS

Although it is difficult to give specific rules for accompanying either a solo voice or a choir, general principles can be stated that provide a useful guide to the young student as he attacks this important problem. Certainly, for the organist who intends to pursue work in a church, no skill is of greater importance than that required for successful performance of vocal and choral accompaniments.

Accompanying the individual voice offers many challenges for you. One of the foremost principles is not to overplay when accompanying a soloist. This is not to suggest leaving a soloist stranded at points of high climax where a truly full accompaniment is demanded. In general, high vocal registers (soprano and tenor voices) demand a somewhat foundational approach to registration, and lower registers (alto and bass), a somewhat brighter tone. The basic idea is to give support in a tonal mass that will complement the voice rather than compete with it. Exceptions to both these techniques will arise; indeed, almost every solo will contain enough variety of structure in it that varied colors and pitches will be needed for proper performance.

---

[1] A small and inexpensive book that deals in a highly effective way with the myriad problems of hymn playing is *The Organist and Hymn Playing* by Austin C. Lovelace, published by Abingdon Press in 1962.

A knowledge of period and style can be helpful. In the performance of a cantata movement by Buxtehude or Bach, you may wish to aim at proper imitation of orchestral timbres of the original. This may mean going to sources to study the original, as not all editions can be relied upon for the necessary information. Failing artistic means to duplicate properly the original—solo violin parts, oboes, and so on—you had better rely on good *organ tone* and render to the best of your ability the sense of the music. If choice of correct stops, nomenclature wise, means a caricature of the original, it is a mistake to *try* for orchestral effects. Here the use of the expression pedals can be judiciously made, as orchestral means presented more dynamic flexibility than would be called for in a piece conceived for Bach's organ! String tone is not always easy to imitate on the organ; in a day when return to true organ tone has reduced the number of strings in most organs to a few relatively mild stops of diapason-type tone that combine well in ensemble, the securing of a "string" tone to imitate a piece originally performed by stringed instruments may be impossible. String tone available on large instruments with orchestral voices, célestes, and similar effects used for romantic music are all unsuitable for music in baroque style. The original performing group of strings would have had a transparent tone, and the imitation of this on the organ can best be essayed, at least, through use of mild string tone with light diapason tone.

The general range of a voice part in a given work must be considered. Tessitura will affect choice of tone color. A phrase may have to be played with more tone than needed at the start—the expression pedal being somewhat closed—in order to have the required dynamic force for points of climax to follow, where addition of stops would be unmusical. Occasionally in music of recent times one finds such climaxes easily achieved by judicious addition of stops at points musically suitable, and this must be carefully planned and executed for the best effect. The muffled tone achieved by closing expression pedals is, on the whole, less satisfactory than ensembles not requiring complete closing of the boxes. The upper pitches of an ensemble are likely to suffer most by closing of boxes, not only reducing volume of sound but dulling the tone and giving an undesirable effect.

In playing accompaniments you must not overlook effects to be gained by use of clear color, string or string and diapason combinations, flutes, or flute and mutations, an occasional foreboding passage—perhaps an interlude or other organ solo—on the fagotto 16′ and diapason 8′ of the Swell, or low chords on the clarinet. With such color effects one must be sure to clarify and reinforce the meaning of the text and select registers carefully in a way to complement the voice. Here again, color effects are devices for variety or interpretation and cannot substitute for ensemble procedures that are the norm in all good playing.

Some slight *crescendi* can be achieved at times without extreme closing of expression pedals as follows: set up manuals with normal coupling—Swell to Choir, Swell and Choir to Great—using only slightly more tone as you move from Swell to Choir, and later from Choir to Great. This can be most useful where the musical phrases suggest some addition of tone with the buildup. Expression pedals on some or all manuals can be used totally or, better, only partially in this process to gain many different effects.

Do not forget that good change of color can be had from completely avoiding coupling except, perhaps, for pedal needs on small organs. Nothing becomes so readily monotonous as organ playing by one who has forgotten that the Swell to Great coupler can be left off at times.

The register of a given passage must be carefully considered in selecting organ tone. Solo lines in the accompaniment can be rendered best in volume and color with careful consideration of range and suitability of organ stops to the period of music. Good baroque reeds may sound well in chorale preludes conceived for the organ but equally ludicrous when employed in movements written for performance by orchestral instruments. The average clarinet, for example, is a poor choice for the music of Bach as it is a relatively modern organ stop. The krummhorn and rohrschalmei will do little to suggest orchestral instrumental sounds to the listener.

A rather high melody may sound lovely on a single 8′ flute. If the quality of the 8′ is not right, experiment with using the 4′ flute an octave lower than written—assuming it is not a "borrowed" stop. You can often solve color problems by using stops in registers not normally used. Whereas a flute 8' with a nasard 2 2/3' might sound well in middle or soprano registers, the combination may sound offensive in tenor register or lower, where the basic pitch will tend to separate from and become dominated by the mutation and result in obscuring the melody.

Some organists make the bad mistake of throwing célestes into full combinations for which they are not intended. The writer has heard various excuses for this kind of procedure: that in French organs the reeds are always out of tune, so inclusion of a céleste for performing French music may help reproduce those ensembles as they actually sound (as if Franck would not have *preferred* to hear his music on an instrument in tune) ; or again, the music is orchestral, and too acute tuning is not "orchestral" in sound, especially where strings are used in the original. Fiddlesticks! Célestes are simply not properly used in combinations of any great degree of volume, unless you wish an emotionalism that properly belongs outside church music, to say the least.

Other organists go to the opposite limit in saying that one must never use the céleste in accompanying the voice. Neither viewpoint seems right. The writer has never heard a truly good singer who was thrown off pitch by the use of a mild céleste in his accompaniment, and many tender moments in great pieces would be lost without them. The flute céleste with 4' coupler makes an elegant foil for a voice in a soft passage. Try it somewhere in Fauré's "Pie Jesu" from the *Requiem* and see if you cannot stir a few normally rigid souls.

The usual problems of vocal accompaniment have been dealt with: choice of basic ensemble or special colors, clear color versus mixed color, the importance of register consideration in selecting proper stops for any given passage, the need to complement a voice in choosing ensemble tone—all of these will prove helpful to study.

One great problem remains: the change of performing medium from piano to organ. Many orchestral reductions are made for piano and involve problems similar to those inherent in music conceived originally for piano. Needless to say you must have knowledge of harmony and style to cope successfully with the many problems of this nature that arise. What notes can best be omitted; where can you respace to advantage (e.g., where in the original a wide gap

169

exists between parts for right and left hands) ; when should you omit the pedal? These rank in importance with the need for pulling out the right stops at the right times.

The respacing of piano music to make it "sound" on the organ can be accomplished well either through inherent good judgment or perhaps more safely through study. Orchestration techniques and a knowledge of the harmonic series are helpful. The knowledge that wider spaces exist in the lower part of the harmonic series than between notes of the upper partials suggests that similar techniques should be employed in chord spacing. Thickness in lower registers gives muddiness. Often omission of Pedal completely gives a good effect, and if the number of voices demands it, you can play on the Pedal blank, with couplers from manuals to duplicate in pedal parts the sounds of the manuals in use at any given moment. The suggestions about chord spacing apply to the norm, and are not intended to suggest revision of passages where the intent of the composer varies from the norm. Generally speaking, the more exceptional the spacing of a given phrase, the more care one must take in registering the passage.

Another simplification can be made in melodic octave passages by using a 4' coupler and playing the bottom notes of the octaves only. This works fine until you encounter a mixture of octaves with other intervals. If the inner parts can be successfully duplicated elsewhere, the technique will still work; however, especially with a composer like Brahms, such simplification will seldom suffice. In Brahm's music the spacing of chord tones is an essential element of style, and too much tampering with this factor may tend to ruin the original.

On a Sunday morning when your choir does not seem to be able to sing on pitch (perish the thought) and even transposing up or down a half step will not alter the condition, you may try giving them a little unison accompaniment of fairly soft stops. Although not a procedure for general use, this will sometimes solve a great problem and avoid the catastrophic results of really flatting in the service. You can simplify your task by using pedal, but blank with only manuals coupled. Quite some years ago Dr. Sowerby jokingly told the writer that when his choir would flat while singing some *a cappella* item during a service, he would enter on the organ, following the number with some ambiguous tonal phrase in low register, probably chromatic in nature, to get back into whatever key might be next required in the service. By this means, also, he served notice to the singers that they had slipped in pitch. Fortunately the writer never had the opportunity of hearing such an occurrence in that great musician's services, but has used the technique in his own service when the unhappy condition of flatting had occurred! It works quite well.

Special color effects—célestes, tremulants, vox humana, and the like—are even less frequently usable in choral accompaniments than in those designed for solo. Tasteful use of tremulant in introductory passages in music of romantic character can give a refreshing change where level of volume will not permit change of stops to secure needed variety. Foundation stops, light mixtures and reeds, are the basic material of which good choral accompaniments are made. Once more, do not overlook the variety to be gained from *terraced dynamics* and the contrast to be gained in passages which use coupling and those that do not.

24

ARTICULATION IN ORGAN PLAYING

Proper execution of repeated notes is a basic essential of good organ playing. Since the release of a note is heard as clearly as the attack—a factor not common to piano playing—this release must be accurate and in accord with firmly established rules. Basic are the following academic rules:

Repeated Notes

1. A repeated note is held for half its normal value.
2. The dot following a repeated note is replaced by a rest.
3. A tied, repeated note is replaced by a rest. (Do not confuse this with an ordinary tied note, as at *a*).

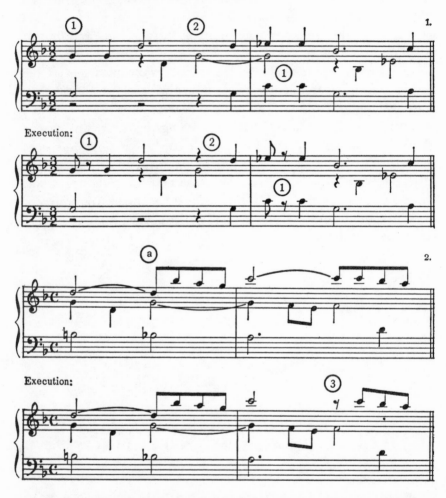

4. Rules 1, 2, and 3 can be abridged for reasons of accent, phrasing, or tempo. Exceptions follow.

[1] Johann Sebastian Bach, "Canzona," *Complete Organ Works,* eds. Widor and Schweitzer (New York: G. Schirmer, Inc., 1912-13), II, 75.
[2] *Ibid.,* p. 72.

These basic rules apply for moderate or fast tempos. As the tempo of a composition becomes slower, the release may become one quarter instead of one half the value of the note. In the examples from "O Mensch, bewein' " given below, the performer may consider the sixteenth note the unit of measure, this being the most frequently occuring note of short duration, and the release of the quarter note is for a sixteenth rest instead of an eighth; see 1a. Other instances may require reduction to a thirty-second rest. The importance of the

dissonances created (as shown in the last two examples) to the expressive quality of this music requires the alteration of rule 3 as shown in 3a. The same applies to rules 1 and 2. You have seen examples where the release is one half and one quarter the value of a note. In a triple rhythm the release may be one third the value of the repeated note or the value of the unit of rhythm. See example 1a.

[3] Bach, "O Mensch, bewein' dein' Sünde gross," *Organ Works* (Leipzig: Breitkopf und Härtel, 1902) , VII, 48-49.
    [4] *Ibid.*

In general, rhythmic motion takes precedence over stationary notes for the obvious reason that the ear carries through the harmonic sounds until some change of harmony is indicated, but a rhythmic interruption may spoil the essential continuity so characteristic of Bach's music. One solution is formulated in this rule:

5. When a melodic line approaches a unison stepwise, the stationary note must be released before restriking; the length of the release

[5] Bach, "In dulci jubilo," ed. Straube, *Organ Works* (Leipzig: Peters, 1928), V, 38.
[6] "Herr Christ, der ein'ge Gottes-Sohn," *ibid.*, p. 25.

will be for the basic unit of the moving line (usually the common short note of the composition) .

6. When a repeated note appears first in one voice with its repetition occurring in another voice, it is normally tied. Exceptions to this rule are numerous. Some of them are as follows:

6a. If the repetition brings in an important motive or thematic idea, the repeated note may be shortened as indicated by the basic rhythm of the composition. In example 6a below, the note a on the fourth beat of the soprano is broken for this reason; it is, additionally, "phrased" as the last note of the soprano motive.

6b. The phrasing of a motive, as suggested in the preceding paragraph, always takes precedence over the tying of a common tone between two voices; see 6b. In fact, analysis of the excerpt from "Alle Menschen müssen sterben" below, noting the basic rhythmic motive entering in the pedal on the second and third beats, might

---

[7] Cesar Franck, "Chorale in A Minor" (Paris: Durand, n.d.) , p. 3.
[8] "Fugue in D Minor," *Complete Organ Works, op. cit.,* II, 9.

9. Possible execution:

better indicate a rendering of the phrasing as shown above in 6*bb*.

6*c*. When the repeated note shifts from soprano to alto it is usually tied, but when from alto to soprano it is generally detached; see 6*c*. This suggests that the articulation of the main part is given precedence over the secondary part. That is, if the articulation breaks the soprano part, a phrasing of the melodic line must be the performer's intention. Ordinarily the alto can be tied over to give a good legato effect without disturbing the rhythmic character of that line. Such reasoning applies to hymn playing.

10. Execution:

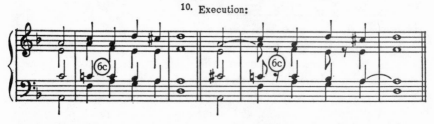

9 "Alle Menschen müssen sterben," *Organ Works* (Breitkopf und Härtel), VII, 4.
10 "Christian, dost thou see them," *Service Book and Hymnal*, Lutheran, No. 68, First Tune, Augsburg.

6d. Similar cases are decided on the basis of harmonic content. When no change of harmony is involved, tying is indicated, but with a change of harmony phrasing the repeated note is often preferable. Note in example 6*c* above there is no change of harmony between the first two beats of M. 2, and yet a break *is* indicated; the legato in the outer voices gives continuity, and detaching the repeated notes creates a feeling of forward motion, quite essential in good hymn playing.

6e. The following example illustrates clearly that preservation of an underlying rhythmic motion can precede in importance the holding of principal melodic tones.

11. Execution:

Phrasing

The "life blood" of good organ playing is intelligent phrasing. Excessively detached playing or completely legato playing leads to a dull result. This means that all techniques producing a good legato are basic to good playing, as is careful attention to the varied detached touches indicated by musical context of a given composition.

7. Special legato techniques commonly used in organ playing are:
   a) substitution,
   b) crossing over or under of fingers,
   c) ordinary glissando, and
   d) thumb slide (or glissando).

[11] "Lobt Gott, ihr Christen, allzugleich," *Organ Works* (Breitkopf und Härtel), VII, 43.

8. Detached playing involves ordinary staccato (8a, each note receiving one half its normal value) and portato (8b, each note receiving three quarters of its normal value). See illustrations with execution below.

The staccato may be a wrist movement, particularly suitable for rapid or extended passages, or a finger movement that simply involves accurate release of tones after half their normal duration.

9. Entire chords may be detached in strongly rhythmic passages.

10. Pickup chords may be detached to give emphasis to the chord following in strong rhythmic position.

[12] "Fugue in D Minor," *Complete Organ Works, op. cit.,* II, 8.
[13] "Toccata in F Major," *ibid.,* IV, 6-7.

14.

11. The detaching of notes for purposes of phrasing, giving life and interest to the musical idea, is most commonly associated with wide leaps like the octave and fifth (especially descending), but may under special rhythmic circumstances apply even to the interval of the third. A few examples will help to clarify this concept.

11a, b. The following example from "Herr Christ, der ein'ge Gottes Sohn" illustrates the detaching of an octave, the first note of which comes on an accent, the second of which precedes a rest. A second principle is illustrated as well: that long tones in a passage of relatively short tones are often detached. A second illustration is seen in 11b.

11c. On the other hand, where relatively short notes fall in normally strong rhythmic position, these may be detached to emphasize the contradictory character of the melodic-harmonic design. Note that in 11c even the descending fifth has been *connected;* the rhythmic design (emphasis on long tones) takes on greater im-

15.

16.

17.

[14] "Fugue in D Major," *ibid.,* II, 68.
[15] "Herr Christ, der ein'ge Gottes Sohn," *Organ Works* (Breitkopf und Härtel), VII, 27.
[16] "Sonata III," *Complete Organ Works, op. cit.,* V, 87.
[17] Dietrich Buxtehude, "Fugue in F Major," *Ausgewahlte Orgelwerke,* ed. Herman Keller (Leipzig: Peters, 1938), I, 34.

portance than the wide, descending interval (which is often detached).

12. In the final examples given below 12*a* shows a detached fourth. In 12*b* the detached ascending octave emphasizes the strong rhythmic character of the syncopation. 12*c* illustrates the phrasing of an accompaniment motive. In 12*d* the phrasing emphasizes both the syncopation and the upbeat character of the motive. The detached notes in 12*e* clarify the fact that the phrase begins on a fraction of a beat.

[18] "Christ ist erstanden," *Organ Works* (Breitkopf und Härtel), VII, 7.
[19] "Christ lag in Todesbanden," *ibid.*, p. 10.
[20] "Erschienen ist der herrliche Tag," *ibid.*, p. 21.
[21] "Puer natus in Bethlehem," *ibid.*, p. 50.
[22] "Prelude in A Major," *Complete Organ Works, op. cit.*, IV, 54.

25

EARLY HISTORY OF THE ORGAN

An Outline

Legend has maintained that the organ traces its ancestry to the pipes of pan (the *syrinx*), a primitive instrument made of reeds bound together and blown across their end to produce a scale.[1]

The *aulos*, a single or double reed instrument blown through a mouthpiece, was favored by ancient Greeks. Shepherds are known to have played one of the many varieties of *auoli* known as the *askaulos*. It was a combination of double-reed *auoli* with a bellows, similar to that of a bagpipe, to furnish wind.[2]

The ancient Egyptians and Mesopotamians had some kind of organ at a very early date.

The *Cheng*, or *Sheng*, a Chinese instrument known for over five thousand years, consisted of reeds standing in a cluster on a bowl, or wind-chest, into which wind was blown. To sound a pipe, the player stopped a hole at the base of the instrument.[3]

The water organ, or *hydraulus*, was invented by Ctesibius of Alexandria in the third century, B.C. This instrument is described by Hero in his work *"Pneumatica"* (about 120 B.C.) as a series of pipes standing over a reservoir into which air was pumped. Water was used to stabilize the pressure and air could be admitted to the foot of the pipes by the action of slides or tongues.

The *hydraulus* was a popular instrument in ancient Rome where it was featured at games and sometimes used in homes of the wealthy. Slaves were employed to pump the loud instrument, long regarded by Christians as a pagan device, a fact not difficult to comprehend in the light of the use to which it was put.

[1] Donald N. Ferguson, *A History of Musical Thought* (3rd ed.; New York: Appleton-Century-Crofts, Inc., 1959), pp. 191-92.
[2] *Ibid.* See Finney, *op. cit.,* p. 19.
[3] Sumner, *op. cit.,* p. 16.

The date of the invention of the *pneumatic organ* is not known; however, on an obelisk erected in Byzantium (before A.D. 393) such an instrument is mentioned.[4] Significantly Byzantium became the center of organ building in the Middle Ages. In 757 Constantine V sent an organ from Byzantium to Pepin the Short, giving us the first evidence of the use of a pneumatic organ in Western Europe. The instrument had lead pipes and was installed in the Church of St. Cornelius at Compiègne.[5]

Records tell of one early instrument which, though it had only sixteen pipes, had to be played by six men, two of whom performed and four of whom supplied the necessary wind.

Organ building, according to Sumner, was carried on in England in the early part of the eighth century and was started in France "about the middle of the eighth century." [6] Organs built by Dunstan of Canterbury (925-88) sometimes had pipes of brass, and during its long history the organ has had pipes constructed from all manner of materials including lead, copper, tin, silver, glass, ivory, and various kinds of wood; eventually tin and wood proved to be the most satisfactory materials for that job. Progress in organ building in Germany dates from the ninth century. We read that in 880 the Pope ordered an organ and builder as well from Germany.

Although the organ had made slow progress in being accepted by the church, once its value was recognized its use spread rapidly. Before the tenth century the organ was generally found only in the palaces of the wealthy or nobility; sometimes in monasteries it was used in giving musical instruction.[7] As time passed monks were frequently found to be organ builders as well as performers on the instrument. "It was not until about the fifteenth century that organ building became a profession." [8]

Early instruments were increased in size, and examples like that built for the cathedral at Winchester, England (about 950), were remarkable indeed. This organ had four hundred pipes, was played

[4] Sumner, *op. cit.*, gives the date as 395. P. 30.
[5] "Organ," *The Columbia Encyclopedia* (2nd ed., 1950), p. 1450.
[6] *Op. cit.*, p. 32.
[7] Finney, *op. cit.*, p. 178.
[8] Barnes, *op. cit.*, p. 13.

by two organists on two keyboards, each of which had twenty slides. There were twenty-six bellows worked by seventy men, and according to accounts the sound must have been so great as to be almost unbearable. This instrument was essentially a mixture organ; that is, when a "key" was depressed it played a given note on each rank of pipes, as no invention to isolate individual ranks had as yet been introduced. For many years such large instruments as this were not commonplace. Most instruments belonged to one of two categories, the portative or the positive.

The *portative* organ was so named because it was movable and could be carried and played in processions. It was sometimes used for support of plainsong.

The *positive* organ, though ordinarily movable, was an "organ in position" due to its augmented size. It also furnished choir accompaniment.

Up until the eleventh century, tongues (*linguae*) at the base of pipes were moved horizontally to cut off or admit wind to the pipes. At this time vertically operated wooden levers, operating on valves inside the chests, were substituted for the earlier mechanisms.[9] In Sumner we read that keyboards were in use before the twelfth century, and it seems reasonable that the eleventh-century date is correct.[10] The first "keys" were heavy and clumsy and had to be struck by the fist. They were also sometimes quite large, having a width of three to six inches.[11] An organ built in Halberstadt in 1381 had three manual keyboards and a pedal keyboard constructed with the same arrangement of white and black notes as is used today.[12] It was not until around 1500 that the keys of the organ reached the approximate size used today.[13]

Another type of small organ not previously mentioned was the *regal* (thought to have been invented about 1450). In this instru-

[9] Emanuel Winternitz, "The Early History of the Organ," *The Organ*, Columbia Record DL 5288, p. 10. Willi Apel, "Organ," *Harvard Dictionary of Music* (Cambridge: Harvard University Press, 1944), p. 531, gives the date for substitution of these primitive "key mechanisms" for the tongues as the thirteenth century.

[10] *Op. cit.*, p. 55.

[11] Barnes, *op. cit.*, quotes Stainer, p. 12.

[12] *The Columbia Encyclopedia, op. cit.*, p. 1450.

[13] Barnes, *op. cit.*, p. 12.

ment reeds replaced flues. The regal gained popularity in part due to the fact that it would stay in tune better than an organ with flue pipes when subjected to fluctuations of wind pressure. Reed pipes were introduced into organs other than regals, and the word "regal" became a generic term for the short resonator reeds (a category of reeds called schnarrwerk from their rattling sounds) .[14]

Still later, with the addition of flues, or resonators, to them, regals developed into a completely new category of reed instruments shaped like the trumpet of today's organ.

In 1550 George Voll of Nuremberg made a regal shaped like a large book; it could be closed after use.

Up to the fourteenth century, as noted above, organs were mixtures due to the fact that when a key was depressed, all pipes connected therewith sounded at once. The Halberstadt organ, with its three manual keyboards, went a long way toward adding new variety. The next invention however, that gave new impetus to development of the organ was the *slide* by means of which the wind supply to any rank of pipes could be opened or closed at will. With this dramatic new feature, interest in many new varieties of stops was created. Pipes were given varied scalings.[15] Stopped and partially stopped pipes were created and eventually many different reed voices were introduced into the organ.[16] For the first time, 16′ and 32′ pipes were built, and these required extra wind supply. Hand-pumped organs gave way in large to those with bellows that could be treaded. This transition represents the change that took place in the Late Gothic organ as it developed into the Renaissance organ.[17]

Invention of pedals is attributed to Albert Van Os (about 1120) ; to one Van Valbeke of Brabant; and to a German named Bernhard (1470), an organist in Venice. Obviously the work of many men, the Pedal "organ" began as a pulldown mechanism permitting the operating of low keys of the manual by the feet.

[14] These reeds featured many and varied shapes from which they were often named.

[15] There was much experimentation with thin-scaled (male or *männerlich*) and wide-scaled (female or *weiblich*) flues.

[16] Apel says that reeds were introduced into the organ in the sixteenth century. *Op. cit.,* p. 633.

[17] See the chapter on German organ music, p. 96.

About 1418 the pedals began to be attached to independent pedal pipes. The earliest music in which a pedal part is indicated is that written by a monk, Adam Ilegorgh; the tablatures date from 1448. After 1475 all important organs were built with "pedalboards" of some type. For further information see the chapters on Italian, Spanish, English, and German music.

It is especially interesting to note the varied directions taken in development of the *Pedal organ*. South German organ development, being influenced by the Italian school of building, featured little use of the pedal, but in north Germany, Pedal divisions grew to quite large size and furnished an essential part of the instrument for which Bach's music was written. The English were particularly slow to develop the Pedal organ, though it was here that the radiating and concave pedal board—in general use today, especially in England and America—was developed in stages by Elliot and Hill (1829), Schulze (1851) and finally S. S. Wesley and Father Willis (1855).[18]

Credit for developing the *Swell organ* is most frequently given to Abraham Jordan for a device he invented in 1712. We know, however, that experiments in that direction had been made elsewhere at an earlier date. Geer notes that the Organo Grande of the Toledo Cathedral, built in the latter half of the seventeenth century, had an enclosed division.[19]

Mechanical Controls

Control of the ever-increasing tonal resources of the organ has been made possible through the *ventil system* and through "a system of combination pistons improved by Henry Willis."[20] With these the organist can change stops by pressing a button.

It was Spackman Barker who, about 1832, invented the so-called *Barker lever*. He made "a small bellows that would rise when a key was pressed down and do the work of moving the entire weight of the action to the pallet (controlling admission of air to the pipes)."[21]

[18] Goode, Jack C., "Organ," *The American People's Encyclopedia* (New York: Grolier Incorporated, 1964), XIV, 891.

[19] *Op. cit.*, p. 239.

[20] Goode, *op. cit.*, p. 891.

[21] *Ibid.*

"In 1867 the work of Spackman Barker was applied by Henry Willis in a practical way in *Tubular-pneumatic* action, taking much of the hard work out of organ playing. Later developments in actions were *electro-pneumatic* and *direct electric*." [22]

It is interesting to note at this writing that there is a trend back to the use of tracker action in pipe organ construction. There is a renewed interest, too, in baroque stops and pipe ranks that have a pronounced chiff. Effort has been made to return to a more traditional organ ensemble than that which developed in the romantic school, but there are various schools of thought; it would probably be, to say the least, unwise to hazard a guess as to where it will all end. One thing is sure, the organ is a powerful and undying instrument to create so many rabid zealots for its various manifestations today.

[22] *Ibid.*

Bibliography

Books

Apel, Willi, editor. *Harvard Dictionary of Music.* Cambridge, Mass.: Harvard University Press, 1944.

Barnes, William Harrison. *The Contemporary American Organ: Its Evolution.* Seventh Edition. Glen Rock, N. J.: J. Fischer & Bro., 1959.

Bedbrook, Gerald Stares. *Keyboard Music from the Middle Ages to the Beginnings of the Baroque.* London: Macmillan & Co., Ltd., 1949.

Bonavia-Hunt, Noel A. *The Modern British Organ.* Revised Edition. London: A. Weekes & Co., n.d.

Chase, Gilbert. *The Music of Spain.* New York: Dover Publications, Inc., 1959.

Dufourcq, Norbert. *La Musique d'Orgue Française.* Second Edition. Paris: Librairie Floury, 1949.

Erné, Lambert. *Dispositien der Merkwaardigste Kerk-Orgelen, door Joachim Hess.* Utrecht: J. A. H. Wagenaar, 1945.

Ewen, David, editor. *European Composers Today: A Biographical and Critical Guide.* New York: The H. W. Wilson Co., 1954.

Ferguson, Donald Nivison. *A History of Musical Thought.* Third Edition. New York: Appleton-Century-Crofts, Inc., 1959.

Finney, Theodore Mitchell. *A History of Music.* Revised Edition. New York: Harcourt, Brace & Co., 1947.

Geer, E. Harold. *Organ Registration in Theory and Practice.* Glen Rock, N. J.: J. Fischer & Bro., 1957.

Germani, Fernando. *Method for the Organ.* Rome: Edizioni de Santis, 1953. Part IV.

Gleason, Harold. *Method of Organ Playing.* Fourth Edition. New York: Appleton-Century-Crofts, Inc., 1949.

Grace, Harvey. *The Organ Works of Bach.* London: Novello & Co., Ltd., 1951.

Hughes, Rupert. *Music Lover's Encyclopedia.* Compiled and edited by Deems Taylor and Russell Kerr. New York: Garden City Publishing Co., 1939.

Hull, A. Eaglefield. *Bach's Organ Works*. London: Musical Opinion, 1929.

Irwin, Stevens. *Dictionary of Pipe Organ Stops*. New York: G. Schirmer, Inc., 1962.

Kinsky, Georg et al, editors. *A History of Music in Pictures*. New York: Dover Publications, 1951.

Koch, Caspar Petrus. *The Organ Student's Gradus ad Parnassum*. New York: J. Fischer & Bro., 1945. Book I.

Locher, Carl. *Die Orgel-Register und Ihre Klangfarben*. Bern: Emil Baumgart, 1904.

Niemann, Walter. *Brahms: A Study of His Life and Work*. Translated by Catherine Alison Phillips. New York: Tudor Publishing Co., 1945.

Peeters, Flor. *Ars. Organi*. Brussels & Paris: Schott Frères, 1953. Part I.

Spitta, Phillipp. *Johann Sebastian Bach: His Work and Influence of the Music of Germany*. 3 vols. Translated by Clara Bell and J. A. Fuller-Maitland. New York: Dover Publications, Inc., 1951.

Sumner, William Leslie. *The Organ: Its Evolution, Principles of Construction and Use*. London: Macdonald & Co., 1952. Also used: Third Edition (revised and enlarged), April 1962.

Trevor, C. H. "The Organ Music of Max Reger and Its Performance," *Organ and Choral Aspects and Prospects*. Edited by Max Hinrichsen. New York: Hinrichsen, 1958.

Westerby, Herbert. *The Complete Organ Recitalist: International Repertoire Guide*. London: The New Temple Press, n.d.

Whitworth, Reginald. *Organ Stops and Their Use*. London: Sir Isaac Pitman & Sons, 1956.

Williams, C. F. Abdy. *The Story of Organ Music*. London: The Walter Scott Publishing Co., Ltd., 1905.

Articles and Pamphlets

Goode, Jack C. "Organ," *American Peoples Encyclopedia*. New York: Grolier Incorporated, 1964, XIV, 890-94.

Herrenschwand, Franz. "The Organ Music of Max Reger," *The American Organist*. New York, March, 1961, pp. 13-14.

Meli, Ernesto. "La Ricerca e la Tutela Degli Organi Storici ed Artistici Nella Regione Lombarda," *L'Organo*. Brescia, 1960. Vol. I.

Tuthill, Burnet C. "Leo Sowerby," *The Musical Quarterly*. New York: G. Schirmer, Inc., July, 1938, pp. 249-64.

Record Albums

Biggs, E. Power. "Notes," *Organ Music of Spain and Portugal.* Columbia Record Album, COL. 5167.

Winternitz, Emanuel. "The Early History of the Organ," from Columbia Record Album, DL 5288.

Music

Ahrens, Joseph. *Christus Ist Erstanden.* Mainz: B. Schott's Söhne, 1935.

———. *Concertino für Positiv.* Heidelberg: Willy Müller, Süddeutscher Musikverlag, 1953.

———. *Das Heilige Jahr.* Heidelberg: Willy Müller, Süddeutscher Musikverlag, 1953. Heft I.

———. *Lobe den Herren.* Mainz: B. Schott's Söhne, 1936.

———. *Triptychon über B-A-C-H.* Mainz: B. Schott's Söhne, 1949.

Bach, Johann Sebastian. *Complete Organ Works.* Edited by Charles Marie Widor and Albert Schweitzer. New York: G. Schirmer, Inc., 1912-13. Vols. I-V.

———. *Oeuvres complètes pour orgue.* Edited by Marcel Dupré. Paris: S. Bornemann, 1940. Vol. VIII.

———. *Organ Works.* Edited by Karl Straube. Leipzig: C. F. Peters, 1928. V, VI, 131.

———. *Organ Works.* Leipzig: Breitkopf und Härtel, 1902. Vol. VII.

———. *Twelve Chorale Preludes by J. S. Bach.* Edited by Franklin Glynn. New York: G. Schirmer, Inc., 1931.

Biggs, E. Power, editor. *Treasury of Early Organ Music.* New York: Mercury Music Corporation, 1947.

Bijster, Jacob. *Variaties op een Oud-Nederlandsch Lied.* Amsterdam: Metro Muziek, n.d.

Bingham, Seth. *Armonie di Firenze.* New York: G. Schirmer, Inc., 1929.

———. "Sonata of Prayer and Praise." New York: H. W. Gray Co., 1959.

Bonnet, Joseph, editor. *Historical Organ-Recitals.* New York: G. Schirmer, Inc., 1917, 1945. Vols. I, VI.

Brahms, Johannes. *Eleven Chorale Preludes.* Edited by Stuart Archer. London: W. Paxton & Co., Ltd., 1929.

Buxtehude, Dietrich. *Ausgewählte Choralbearbeitungen.* Edited by Hermann Keller. Leipzig: C. F. Peters, 1938.

———. *Ausgewählte Orgelwerke.* Edited by Hermann Keller. Leipzig: C. F. Peters, 1938.

Campbell, Sidney S., transcriber. *Three 18th Century Voluntaries.* London: Oxford University Press, 1956.

De Klerk, Albert. *Ricercare voor Orgel*. Utrecht: Wed. J. R. Van Rossum, 1951.

DeLamarter, Eric. "A Gothic Prelude." New York: G. Schirmer, Inc., 1937.

————. "Festival Prelude." New York: Whitmark & Sons, 1945.

————. *Suite for Organ*. New York: Whitmark & Sons, 1945.

Demessieux, Jeanne. *Sept meditations sur le Saint Esprit*. Paris: Durand, 1947.

————. *Twelve Choral Preludes*. Boston: McLaughlin & Reilly, 1950.

Dragt, Jaap. *3 Koraalpreludes*. Goes: Ars Nova, 1958.

————. *5 Koraalpreludes*. Amsterdam: G. Alsbach & Co., n. d.

Dufourcq, Norbert, editor. *The Paris Organ During the Reign of Louis XIV*. Copenhagen: Wilhelm Hansen, 1956.

Franck, César. "Chorale in A Minor." Paris: Durand, n. d.

————. *Organ Works*. New, York: G. Schirmer, Inc., 1925.

Frescobaldi, Girolamo. *Ausgewählte Orgelwerke in Zwei Bänden*. Edited by Hermann Keller. Leipzig: C. F. Peters, 1943.

Fuser, Ireneo, editor. *Classici Italiani dell' Organo*. Padova, Italy: Edizioni Zanibon, 1955.

Handel, George Frederick. *G. F. Haendel: Seize Concertos*. Edited by Marcel Dupré. Paris: S. Bornemann, 1937. Vols. I, II.

————. *Orgel Konzert Nr. I, g-moll*. Kassel und Basel: Bärenreiter, 1948.

Hindemith, Paul. "Sonate I." London: Schott & Co., Ltd., 1937.

————. "Sonate II." Mainz: B. Schott's Söhne, 1937.

————. "Sonate III." Mainz: B. Schott's Söhne, 1940.

Howell, Almonte C., Jr., editor. *Five French Baroque Organ Masses*. Lexington: University of Kentucky Press, 1961.

Howells, Herbert. *Three Psalm-Preludes*. London: Novello and Co., Ltd., 1940, 1949. Sets I, II.

Karg-Elert, Sigfrid. "Cathedral Windows," *Six Pieces on Gregorian Tunes*. London: Elkin & Co., Ltd., 1923.

————. *Chorale Improvisations*. New York: E. B. Marks, 1941. Opus 65. Vols. IV, VI.

————. *Seven Chorale Improvisations*. London: W. Paxton & Co., Ltd., 1909. Opus 65.

Kee, Cor. *Psalmen voor Orgel*. Amsterdam: G. Alsbach & Co., n. d. Band II, Band III.

Kee, Piet. *God Is Tegenwoordig*. Goes: Ars Nova, 1953.

Langlais, Jean. *Hommage à Frescobaldi*. Paris: S. Bornemann, 1952.

————. *Suite brève*. Paris: S. Bornemann, 1947.

————. *Suite française*. Paris: S. Bornemann, 1949.

————. *Suite médiévale.* Paris: Editions Salabert, 1950.

Liszt, Franz. *Orgelkompositionen.* Edited by Karl Straube. New York, London, Frankfurt: C. F. Peters, n. d. Vols. I, II.

Mendelssohn-Bartholdy, Felix. *Organ Works.* Edited by Lemare, New York: G. Schirmer, Inc., 1910.

Messiaen, Olivier. *Apparition de l'église éternelle.* Paris: Lemoine, 1934.

————. *La nativité du seigneur.* Paris: Leduc, 1936.

Mulet, Henry. *Esquisses Byzantines.* Paris: Leduc, 1920.

Muset, Joseph, editor. *Early Spanish Organ Music.* New York: G. Schirmer, Inc., 1948.

Peeters, Flor. *30 Chorale Preludes on Gregorian Hymns.* New York: C. F. Peters, 1955. Opus 76.

————. *30 Chorale Preludes on Well-Known Hymn Tunes.* New York: C. F. Peters, 1950. Opus 70.

Pepping, Ernst. *Grosses Orgelbuch.* Mainz: B. Schott's Söhne, 1941. Teil III.

Phillips, Gordon, editor. *Tallis to Wesley.* New York, London, Frankfurt: Peters & Hinrichsen Edition, 1958, 1957. Nos. 4, 9.

Post, Piet. "Canonische Variaties over 'Als God, mijn God, maar voor mij is.' " Goes: Ars Nova, 1955.

————. "Partite Diverse Sopra Ps. 101." Goes: Ars Nova, n. d.

————. "Partita over de Avondzang." Goes: Ars Nova, 1956.

————. "Psalm 84." Goes: Ars Nova, 1951.

Purcell, Henry. *Ceremonial Music for Organ.* Edited by E. Power Biggs. New York: Mercury Music Corporation, 1946.

————. *Henry Purcell—Organ Works.* Edited by Hugh McLean. London: Novello & Co., Ltd., 1957.

Reger, Max. *Zwölf Stücke für die Orgel.* Leipzig: C. F. Peters, 1929. Opus 59. Vols. I, II.

Reubke, Julius. "The 94th Psalm Sonata." New York: G. Schirmer, Inc., 1934.

Schumann, Robert. *Sechs Fugen über den Namen B-a-c-h.* Leipzig: Peters, n. d. Opus 60.

Senn, Jurt Wolfgang; Schmid, Wilhelm; and Aeschbacher, Gerhard; editors. *Orgelchoräle des 17. und 18. Jahrhunderts.* Basel & Kassel: Bärenreiter, 1950.

Sowerby, Leo. "Ballade for English Horn & Organ." New York: H. W. Gray Co., 1950.

————. "Comes Autumn Time." Boston: The Boston Music Co., 1927.

————. *Festival Musick.* New York: H. W. Gray Co., 1958.

———. "Holiday Trumpets" from album "The Colours of the Organ." London: Novello and Co., Ltd., 1960.

———. "Jubilee." New York: H. W. Gray Co., 1959.

———. "Prelude on 'Capel.' " New York: H. W. Gray Co., 1956.

———. "Prelude on 'Charterhouse.' " New York: H. W. Gray Co., 1956.

———. "Requiescat in Pace." New York: H. W. Gray Co., 1926.

———. "Sonatina." New York: H. W. Gray Co., 1947.

———. *Symphony in G. Major*. London: Oxford University Press, 1932.

———. "Toccata." New York: H. W. Gray Co., 1941.

———. "Whimsical Variations." New York: H. W. Gray Co., 1952.

Stanley, John. *Suite for Organ*. London: Oxford University Press, 1945.

Straube, Karl, editor. *Alte Meister des Orgelspiels*. Leipzig: C. F. Peters, 1929.

Tallis, Thomas. *Thomas Tallis—Complete Keyboard Works*. Edited by Denis Stevens. New York, London, Frankfurt: Peters & Hinrichsen Edition, 1953.

Van der Horst, Anthon. *Suite in Modo Conjuncto*. Goes: Ars Nova, 1945.

Vierne, Louis. *24 Pièces en style libre*. Paris: Durand, 1914. Book II.

———. *24 Pièces de fantaisie*. Paris: Henry Lemoine & Cie., 1926-27. Suites I, III, IV.

———. *Deuxième Symphonie*. Paris: J. Hamelle, 1903.

———. *First Symphony*. New York: E. B. Marks, 1946.

———. *6me Symphonie*. Paris: Lemoine, 1931.

Widor, Charles Marie. *Fifth Symphony*. New York: E. B. Marks, 1936.

———. *Symphonie IV*. Paris: Hamelle, n. d.

Dictionary of Stops

The following is a list of abbreviations used: D. Dutch, E. English, F. French, G. German, Gk. Greek, I. Italian, L. Latin, S. Spanish, and the sign = indicates literal meaning of the term. German nouns, usually capitalized, are given in lowercase for ease in reading.

acoustic bass. 32′. A resultant tone, combining a 16′ pedal stop with another rank of 10 2/3′. May be open or stopped pipes. In contemporary practice the two ranks are usually drawn separately to form the "synthetic" 32′ effect.

acuta. (L. *acutus*=sharp) G. akuta or scharf. High-pitched mixture containing a third-sounding rank.

aeoline. L. aeolina, G. äoline, F. éoline. 8′. Soft stop.

aeoline céleste. 8′. Two ranks of soft strings, one tuned slightly sharp to give an undulating effect.

aeolsharfe. (Aeolian harp) 4′ aeoline. Also in G. usage a reed, e.g., äolinenbass 16′ for dulcianbass.

aliquot. G. Partial or overtone.

altra vigesima seconda. (I.=another twenty-second) Used for a flute stop when forming a cornet.

amorosa. I. See FLÛTE D'AMOUR (F). Also FLAUTO AMABILE (I).

a(o)lodicon. Term used in G. organs for dulcian.

apfelregal. (G.=apple reed) Also called knopfregal. 8′. Ancient reed stop with short, apple-shaped resonators.

aukustich. G. A rare acoustic 64′ formed from combination of 32′ and 21 1/3′ ranks.

baarpijp. (D.=bear pipe) G. bärpfeife. 8′, 4′. Rough-sounding reed, stopped. Gross bearpipen 16′ also found.

bachflöte. 2′. See GEMSHORN.

bajon. S. Bassoon.

bariton. Also baryton. 8′ baritone. Commonly used for heavy pedal reed. Also used for tenor vox humana and tenor viola (viola di bordone).

basse harmonique. See ACOUSTIC BASS.

basse ouverte. (F.=open bass) Equivalent to G. flötenbass, generally indicating a register of more definitive pitch than the subbass.

basset-horn. I. corno di bassetto. 8′. Clarinet-like solo reed. Also used at 16′ pitch for pedal or solo stop. Exceptional G. usage *may* indicate closed flue of small scale.

bassflöte. G. Also flötbass or flötenbass. While "bass" usually signifies a 16′ register, this stop is often an 8′ open wood stop.

bass flute. Term suggests an 8′ extension of a 16′ bourdon.[1] See BASSFLÖTE.

basson-hautbois. F. Bassoon-oboe. A single stop. See BASSOON.

bassoon. G. fagott, F. basson, S. bajon, I. fagotto. 16′, 8′, 4′. Stopped reed, imitative quality but a good ensemble stop, especially in the 16′ pitch as contra-fagotto or fagotto.

bauerflöte. (G.=peasant flute) Also bauernflöte. 8′, 4′, 2′, 1′. Flute of small scale. As pedal 2′, sometimes bauer pfeiffe.

bayerflöit bass. G. 1′ pedal stop of bourdon category.

bell diapason. F. flûte à pavillon. A loud flute tone produced by diapason pipes having a flared cone on top.

bell gamba. E. Now obsolete. String with conical bell. Small scaled.

bifara. I. Open flue with two mouths giving undulating effect. Examples constructed with two ranks of single-mouth design. Although Germani calls the piffaro a "diapason celeste," Sumner says that bifara and piffaro are of the same class.[2]

blochflöte. G. Also blockflöte, plockpfeiffe. The recorder. An imitative flute stop.

bombarde. F. (1) Organ division. (2) Loud free reed of 32′, 16′, and 8′ pitches. Name derived from ancient instrument.[3]

bombardon. 32′, 16′. Pedal reed of tone quality between that of the bombarde and bassoon.

bommart. G. Also bombart. 16′, 8′. Stopped reed.

bourdon. (F. *bourdonner*=to buzz) G. bordun (also F.) or brummbass, I. bordone. 16′ flue, stopped. Also 32′ and 8′.

bratsche. G. Viola. A flue.

buccina. I. Seldom used name for loud chorus reed of trombone character.

buzian. D. 32′, 16′. See POSAUNE.

calcantenglocke. (G=tread bell) Used to signal bellows treader.

campanelli. I. Also campana. G. glöcklein. High-pitched stop repeating in each octave. Combined with other stops to give a bell-like sound. Also campanette, campanilla, or zimbelflöte.[4]

carillon. (1) Commonly a set of tubular bells sounding when struck by hammers. (2) A two- to six-rank mixture with octave-, fifth-, and prominent third-sounding ranks, so named as it has a bell-like sound.

celesta. 4′. Metal plates sounded by hammers.

céleste. F. Compound stop with two ranks of identical scaling and quality, one rank being tuned slightly sharp, or flat, to the regular-tuned rank, thus creating an undulating effect.

celestina. I. Soft wood flute, open, of small scale.

cello. 8′. Also violoncello. A foundational string.

chalumeau. F. G. schalmei, E. shawn. 8′. Mild reed made in imitation of the shawn, the father of the clarinet. At 4′ it may be part of a bright reed chorus.

[1] Sumner, *op. cit.*, p. 276.

[2] *Ibid.*, p. 277.

[3] *A History of Music in Pictures*, ed. Georg Kinsky. (New York: Dover Publications, 1951), p. 148.

[4] Stevens Irwin. *Dictionary of Pipe Organ Stops*. (New York: G. Schirmer, Inc., 1962), p. 43.

chamade. F. Term applied to horizontally placed reed, e.g., trompette en chamade. Often though not always displayed in the organ case.

chimney flute. F. flûte à cheminée, G. rohrflöte or rohrschelle. A stop with many varied forms, often capped, with a small tube through the cap, hence a partially stopped pipe.

choral bass. 4'. Bright open pedal stop. Also a 2' register.

clairon. F. See CLARION.

clarabella. (I.=bright bell) 8', 4'. Bright solo wood stop. Generally does not blend well in ensemble.

claribel flute. 8', 4'. Open wood stop.

clarinet. I. clarinetto. 8'. Good imitative solo reed. Sometimes used at 16' pitch.

clarion. 4'. Strong open reed, generally combined with reeds of 16' and 8' to form a reed chorus.

clarion mixture. Strong mixture used in substitution for a Great clarion 4'.

clear flute. G. hellflöte. 4'. Open wood stop.

compensationsmixtur. Rare compound stop of Pedal organ designed to supply pitches required in a pedal ensemble of a particular organ for completeness.

concert flute. Orchestral flute, imitative tone. An open wood stop.

contra. Prefix normally indicating 16' manual or 32' pedal stop.

contrabass. F. contrebass, I. contrabasso. 16'. Strong open flue in Pedal, imitative of the double bass.

contraposaune. (G.=double trombone) 16' manual, 32' pedal register.

coppel. G. Also koppel or coppelflöte. Open metal flute, useful in combination, especially with mutations.

copula. (L.=a coupler) A stop that has as its purpose the binding together of certain ensemble components.[5]

cor anglais. I. corno inglese. 8'. See ENGLISH HORN.

cor de nuit. F. G. nachthorn or waldflöte. 8', 4', 2', 1'. A wide-scaled, quiet flue with somewhat reedy tone. Generally open, though sometimes stopped pipes.

cordedain. Terminology used by Silbermann for soft 4' flute.

cornet. F. Name applied to a solo mixture—generally flute but rarely dulciana or viol ranks are used—or to combination formed by drawing the following flute ranks: 8', 4', 2 2/3', 2', 1 3/5'. The third-sounding rank is essential; the 4' or 2' rank *may* be omitted. As a mixture designed for solo use, the stop contains no breaks. Not to be confused with the G. cornett.

cornett. G. 4', 2'. Term sometimes used today is "singend cornett." Also cornet-tino (2' manual) and cornett bass (4' or 2' pedal). Open solo pedal reed.

corno d'amore. I. F. cor d'amour. 8' solo reed, usually soft.

corno di bassetto. I. 16'. 8'. In English, a basset horn, solo reed of clarinet category. In G. usage, also a small-scaled flue.

corno dolce. I. 16', 8'. Rare open flue of delicate tone.

corno flute. (1) Soft reed. (2) Open metal flue changing from flute tone in upper compass to a horn-like tone in its tenor register.

cornomeuse. I. Rare stop made to imitate the bagpipes.

cornopean. (L. *cornu*=horn and E. "paean") 8'. Smooth-toned ensemble reed. Terminology less in use by present builders than in previous decades.

[5] *Ibid.,* p. 58.

cremona. Corruption of "krummhorn," used to denote a coarse clarinet. Also a mild violin or viola 8'.[6]

cromorne. F. G. krummhorn, I. cromorno. 8' baroque solo reed. There exists considerable confusion about the meaning and source of this stop name. The G. "krumm" signifies "crooked," and the name logically comes from some type of crooked instrument.

cymbal(e). F. G. zimbel or scharf. A sharp principal mixture containing octave- and fifth-sounding ranks and breaking in each octave; rarely it contains third-sounding ranks.

cymbala. Three bells struck by hammers.

cymbelstern. (G.=cymbal-star). In early organs a wooden star with tiny bells attached to its points, revolving to give a tinkling sound. Sometimes the bells were tuned to harmonic tones. In general the stop is not visible today and may no longer have its original star shape.

decembass. A pedal tièrce.

decima. I. The seventeenth or tenth mutation.

decima nona. I. The nineteenth.

deutsch flöte. G. 8' flute.

diapason. (G.=from the first to the last note) G. prinzipal, F. montre (show pipes), I. principale. Most pitches. Tone peculiar to the organ and distinct in character, somewhere between flute and string tone. This stop varies greatly with country and period of construction.

diapason phonon. Now in disuse by builders, this was a large-scaled stop on high wind pressure created by Robert Hope-Jones.

diaphone. An invention of Hope-Jones, this stop was commonly a valvular foundation rank. John Compton produced varieties in flute, reed, and string categories as well.[7]

diskant mixtur. G. A five-rank pedal stop intended for solo melodies.

dolcan. Soft open, tapered metal flue. Predecessor of the dulciana.

dolce. Soft flue. Tone varied in early G. stops from stringy to horn-like quality.

donner. (G.=thunder) Effect created by sounding large bass pipes simultaneously.

doppelflöte. (G.=double flute) Large-scaled, open flute with a mouth on each of two opposite sides.

doppelgedeckt. G. Similar stop to the doppelflöte but producing a softer tone.

double. Adjective signifying a stop at an octave below its normal register.

doublette. F. 2' flute. The fifteenth. May be a 4' in pedal. A bright sound is created by the two ranks used to create the stop and hence its name.[8]

druckknöpfe. (G.=press buttons) Pneumatic controls for change of combination without disturbing stops drawn at console by the organist.

dulcet. A 4' dulciana.

dulcian. Also dolcian. D. dulciaan. A gentle, stopped reed with small-scaled resonators, generally of wood, used in G. organs.

[6] *Ibid.,* p. 63.
[7] *Ibid.,* p. 74.
[8] *Ibid.,* p. 80.

dulciana. An echo or small-scaled diapason of gentle tone quality, sometimes stringy.

dulciana flute. A hybrid with flute-like tone.

dulciana mixture. Compound stop not in common use today.

dulcimer. Percussion stop using strings. Not a successful invention.

dulzian. G. Also dulzaen. An open flute stop, tapered inward from top to bottom.

duodecima. I. A quint or twelfth mutation.

echo. (1) Adjective denoting a quiet version of a stop. (2) Adjective used to categorize any small-scaled stop such as dulciana or aeoline. (3) An expressive organ division placed at a distance from the main organ and containing soft "color" stops. F. usage in particular in early organs denoted a division in a box, so placed to give an "echo" effect. Sometimes the division was simply placed below the main divisions of the organ to give it a distant effect.

English horn. 8′ Imitative solo reed having a bell on top.

erzähler. G. (*erzählen*=to tell). Stop invented by Ernest M. Skinner in 1904. Though gentle, its gemshorn-like quality is "telling" even in low notes. It makes a fine quality céleste.

euphone. 16′, 8′. Solo reed with smooth quality.

faberton. See CAMPANELLI.

fagott(o). See BASSOON.

feldflöte. G. Also feldpfeife. Flute of penetrating tone. Open or stopped.

fernflöte. G. Echo flute, sometimes tapered like the spitzflöte.

fife. 2′, 1′. Open flute, bright, and not of well-blending qualities.

fiffaro. I. Undulating stop made of quiet, foundational stops and used for expressive passages.[9]

fifteenth. 2′ diapason. The superoctave.

fistula. L. Ancient name for rohrpfeife. Also term used as early as the eleventh century for organ pipes of copper.

flachflöte. G. (*flach*=flat) 8′, 4′, 2′. Open flute, metal or wood, of irregular shape, wide at bottom and narrow at top. Also made in cylindrical shape. Term used with various adjectives: kleinflachflöte 2′, F. discant 2′, grosse F. 8′.

flageolet. (G.=harmonic) 2′, 1′. Open metal flute, quieter than piccolo.

flautada. S. 32′, 16′, 8′. An open, foundational stop of flute-principal hybrid tone.[10]

flautino. (I.=piccolo.) Soft metal flute.

flauto dolce. I. 8′, 4′. Gentle wood flute stop.

flauto major. Open wood flute. Large-scaled clarabella.

flöt(en)bass. G. See BASSFLÖTE.

flügelhorn. 8′. Imitative reed stop named from the alto cornet.

flûte à cheminée. F. See CHIMNEY FLUTE.

flûte à pavillon. F. Hybrid stop. See BELL DIAPASON.

flûte allemande. (F.=German flute)

flûte conique. F. Open, metal flute.

flûte d'amour. (F.=flute of love.) 8′, 4′. Wood flute.

[9] Germani, *op. cit.*, p. 10.
[10] Irwin, *op. cit.*, p. 94.

flûte harmonique. F. See HARMONIC FLUTE.

flötenprinzipal. G. 8'. Principal of flutey character.

fourniture. (F.=furniture) G. mixtur. Compound stop of diapason tone composed of octave- and fifth-sounding ranks.

French horn. 8'. Reed in earlier organs of trumpet- or regal-like tone. Today a soft imitative stop.

fugara. 8', 4'. Open flue of metal or wood with hybrid tone (string-reed or string-diapason quality).

gamba. I. G. F. gambe. Also viola da gamba. Small-scaled open metal stop of string quality. More foundational than the salicional.

gambette. F. An octave gamba.

gedampftregal. (G.=muted regal)

gedeckt. G. Also gedackt. F. bourdon, S. tapada, tapadillo. Stopped flute of wood or metal. Important stop with many varied forms. The rohrgedeckt with its perforated stoppers gives prominent twelfth and seventeenth. The Praetorius table includes the following: subbass 32', gross gedacker, gross gedackt (or grobgedackt), gedackt bass (or gedackt untersatz), klein gedackt, gedacktquinta 3' (2 2/3'). The stopped diapason is also a gedackt type, but has a broader tone than the G. stop.

gedecktpommer. G. Gedeckt overblown to emphasize the twelfth. The word *"pommer"* referring to a G. collective term for early double reeds, suggests a somewhat reedy character. Besides the prominent twelfth (stronger than in the quintaton), its seventeenth may be heard.

geigen. (G. *Geige*=violin) Also geigenprincipal or geigenprinzipal. A violin diapason. Flue with a tone between that of diapason and gamba. Open, metal, having superior blending qualities.

gemshorn. (G.=goat-horn) F. cor de chamois. Open flue (usually metal) of conical shape, tapering toward the top. Common pitches are 8' and 4'. Also used for 32', 2 2/3', and 2'. A well-blending hybrid tone.

glockenspiel. (G.=play of bells) F. carillon, I. campanella. (1) Metal tubes or bars struck by hammers. (2) A sharp mixture.

grand(e). (F.=great) (1) The Great division of a French organ. (2) Ranks of pipes of large scale. (3) A rank whose range is an octave below normal pitch, e.g., a 16' manual or 32' pedal stop.

grand cornet. A cornet based on a 16' manual or 32' pedal series.

gravissima. (L.=the lowest or gravest) Applied to a resultant 64' utilizing a 21 1/3' rank with a 32' rank.

grob or gross. (G.=large) See (2) and (3) under GRAND.

halbprinzipal. (G.=half principal) A 4' stop.

harfenprinzipal. (G.=harp principal) Small-scaled open metal stop intended to imitate the tone of a harp.

harmonia aetheria. (Gk.) A nonbreaking, echo mixture used in German organs, e.g., a two-rank (twelfth and seventeenth) or three-rank (twelfth, fifteenth, and seventeenth).

harmonic. An adjective describing a rank of pipes constructed twice normal length and overblown to speak the first harmonic or octave. Small holes bored at the point of the proper node assist in securing the desired tone. Though full and rich in tone, such stops seldom blend well in ensemble.

harmonic bass. See ACOUSTIC BASS.

harmonic flute. F. flûte harmonique, I. flauto armonico. A flute, often 4', constructed according to principles explained under HARMONIC.

harmonica. Also harmonika. 8'. Small-scaled open flue with tone between that of the aeoline and the salicional.

harmonics. Compound stop often containing third and flat-seventh ranks as well as octaves and fifths.

harp. A percussion stop. Metal or wooden bars with resonators struck by hammers.

hautbois. (F.=high wood [wind]) Oboe. A stop usually located in the Swell or Choir division. Though sometimes of imitative character, it is generally useful in ensemble.

hellflöte. G. (*hell*=bright) Clear-sounding flute.

hohlflöte. G. (*hohl*=hollow) Also hohlpfeife. D. holfluit or holpijp. F. flûte creuse. 16', 8', 4', 2'. Open wood of well-blending quality. Moderately scaled flute.

hohlschelle. (G.=hollow bell) Quintaton type stop now obsolete.

holzgedeckt. Flute 8', 4'. A stopped register made of wood.

horn. (1) Effective imitative reed commonly found in the Solo or Choir division. (2) On Dutch organs, this may indicate a sesquialtera.

horn diapason. A slotted diapason with fine blending qualities.

jubalflöte. G. (*jubal*=joyous) Also seraphonflöte 8', 4'. Open flue having two mouths.

jungfernregal. G. (*Jungfern*=*maiden*) 8' 4'. Soft reed of the schnarrwerk category.

kälberregal. G. (*Kalb*=calf) Archaic reed.

keraulophone. (Gk.=horn and flute) Medium-scaled, cylindrical flute with a perforated tuning slide. Its tone is between that of flute and diapason.

kinura. (G.=a harp) A small-scaled reed of peculiar quality, now fortunately obsolete.

klein. (G.=small) (1) Adjective describing a small-scaled stop. (2) A 4' stop normally built to sound at 8' pitch.

knopfregal. G. (*Knopf*=knob) See APFELREGAL.

koppel. See COPPEL.

krummhorn. See CROMORNE.

kutzialflöte. G. 4', 2', 1', rarely 1 1/3'. Open flute.

larigot. F. (*l'arigot*=slang.) Webster suggests slang as "terms having a forced, fantastic, or grotesque meaning or exhibiting humor or fancy." (The F. term also is for a flageolet.) A mutation sounding the nineteenth. A flute of 2 2/3' in pedal or 1 1/3' in manual divisions. Used to brighten an ensemble or solo combination.

lieblich. (G.=lovely) Adjective signifying a small-scaled, sweet register, e.g., lieblichgedeckt.

lleno. S. (1) Mixture, sometimes of as many as twenty-seven ranks. (2) A full-sounding combination of basic pitch, octaves, and mixtures.

ludwigtone. A complex open stop with two mouths and two vibrating air columns, one tuned sharp, the other flat. In combination with other stops of gentle character it creates a delicate, undulating tone.

lute. See DULCIMER.

major bass. G. untersatz, F. grand bourdon. A 32′ bourdon.

meerflöte. G. (*Meer*=sea) An undulating stop. See UNDA MARIS.

melodia. 8′. Large-scaled, open flute. Does not blend well.

menschenstimme. (G.=human voice). See VOX HUMANA.

messinregal. G. (*messing*=brass) Archaic reed imitative of brass instruments.

mixture. G. mixtur, D. mixtuur, F. mixture, S. lleno, I. ripieno. Compound stop of principal tone, essential to buildup of organ ensemble tone. Harmonics (generally octaves and fifths) forming the stop add brilliance and clarity in middle and low registers but also gravity in high register due to "breaking" of its ranks. Useful for fusing principal and reed tone in ensemble.

montre. F. (*montrer*=to show; the organ display pipes) 32′, 16′, 8′, 4′. Principal type tone.

musette. (F.=bagpipe) G. sackpfeife. 4′. Reed resembling in tone the orchestral oboe.

mutation stops. Stops that alter pitch from the norm, e.g., a nasard (twelfth), tièrce (seventeenth) or larigot (nineteenth).

nachthorn. G. (*Nacht*=night) See COR DE NUIT.

nasard. F. G. nasat, D. nazat, I. and S. nasardo. A mutation of broad scale (flute). Useful in creating synthetic solo voices, e.g., as part of a cornet created by drawing single ranks. Sometimes this stop is one of several hybrid types.

nasardo. S. (1) Compound stop of flute quality. (2) Combination in S. practice which contains quint (s).

nason. 16′, 8′, 4′. Stopped flue with pronounced twelfth and speaking with a chiff.

nineteenth. Member of flue chorus, found often only as one of a mixture's ranks.

oboe. Reed stop generally intended for solo use. See HAUTBOIS.

oboe-flute. Open wood flute of hybrid tone.

oboe horn. Hybrid reed with tone between that of oboe and smooth trumpet. Best use is for solo purposes.

ocarina. 4′. Hollow-toned metal flue. Something of a "freak," according to Sumner.[11]

octavbass. An 8′ principal.

octave. (1) Adjective denoting a 4′ version of an 8′ manual stop. (2) A principal, 4′ manual, or 8′ pedal.

octavin. 2′. Open metal flue of prominent tone.

offenbass. (G.=open bass) A 16′ pedal flue, wood or metal.

open diapason. The diapason or principal has its own color, peculiar to the organ. A nonimitative stop. See PRINZIPAL.

ophicleide. (Gk.=a keyed serpent) Powerful reed stop on high pressure. Named from an ancient brass instrument.

[11] *Op. cit.,* p. 319.

orchestral. Adjective denoting a stop of imitative character. It is well to remember that many stops now in use and considered to have "characteristic organ tone" were, many years ago, named from ancient instruments. Some stops so named are the zink, blockflöte, krummhorn, querflöte, bombard, shawm, and racket, as well as the dolcian, serpent, and ophicleide.

orchestral flute. G. concertflöte, querflöte, wienerflöte, F. flûte traversière, I. flauto traverso. Open, small-scaled flutes built in various shapes, e.g., square, rectangular, and triangular.

orlo. S. 8′ reed of musette type. Also cro orlo.

ottava. I. Octave.

panflöte. 1′. Rare pedal flue named from the mythical Pan's pipes.

pastorita. I. See COR DE NUIT.

pauke. G. (*Pauken*=kettledrums) An old device that used wooden blocks in imitation of a drum.

perduna. I. See BOURDON.

philomela. (1) Sweet-toned, gentle high flue. (2) A loud, double-mouthed open flute.

physharmonika. A stop made from harmonium reeds and using resonators.

piccolo. 2′ flute of open metal or wood pipes.

piffero. (I.=fife). Also piffaro. Terminology used in German building for a bright flute.

pileata. L. A gedeckt.

plein-jeu. F. Chorus mixture of from three to seven ranks of octaves and fifths. Due to breaks, relatively low ranks may occur in the treble.

pommer. See GEDECKT.

portunal. Also bordunalflöte. Open wood flue of reedy quality, made from pyramidal-shaped walls flaring from bottom to top.

posaune. (G.=trombone) Loud reed. Normally 16′ pedal or 8′ manual register.

prestant. F. D. praestant. 4′ diapason. The octave. Terminology also used for 16′ and 8′ stops (D.).

principal. See PRINZIPAL.

prinzipal. G. D. principaal, F. montre, I. principale. A diapason. Though scaling and precise tone color vary with different countries, these are considered equivalents.

prinzipal diskant. An 8′ stop originally used for reinforcement of upper register though now unnecessary due to scaling employed in the diapason chorus.

progressio harmonica. A German mixture whose ranks increased in the upper compass.

pyramidon. Sumner notes this as an unsuccessful attempt to create a 16′ flute from stopped pipes in pyramidal shape.[12]

quarte de nasard. F. The fifteenth, a stop sounding "a fourth above the nasard."

querflöte. (G. *Quer*=cross) I. flauto traverso. The traverse flute of the orchestra.

quincena. S. piccolo.

quint. Also quinte. I, L. qinta. (1) Manual 5 1/3′, pedal 10 2/3′. Mutation suitable with manual 16′. It creates a 32′ resultant combined with pedal 16′.

[12] *Ibid.,* p. 298.

(2) In general organ terminology, any stop sounding a fifth or any given octave thereof.

quintade. 32′, 16′, 8′. Stopped, large-scaled metal flute.

quintadecima. I. The fifteenth.

quintadena. Also quintadeena (D). Diminutive quintaton which, despite size, is generally louder than the quintatön.

quintaten. G. Also quintatön. Stopped flue with prominent twelfth.

rankett. Also racket. Ancient reed named from "orchestral" instrument of bassoon-like character.[13]

rauschflöte. (G.=rustling flute) Also rauschpfeife. S. docena y quincena. Two-rank mixture containing 2′ and 1 1/3′ ranks.

rauschquinte. G. Also rauschpfeife. D. rauschpyp. Two-rank mixture containing 2 2/3′ and 2′ sounding ranks, hence a fourth, causing old German builders to call it quarte or quarta.[14] This stop sometimes contains 1′ and 1 1/3′ ranks, or 1/2′ and 2/3′ ranks.[15]

recorder. Equivalents are G. blockflöte, F. flûte à bec (*beak flute*). Stop imitative of the recorder.

regal. G. F, I. regale, S. regalia. (1) Old reed of the schnarrwerk class. (2) Name given to ancient, small reed organ.

regula. L. Open metal diapason.

reim. Soft 16′ reed. Rare.

ripieno. (I.=filling up) A chorus "mixture" formed by drawing various combinations of the octaves and mutations, ranks of the flue ensemble.

rohrflöte. G. Also rohrschelle. D. roerfluit. See CHIMNEY FLUTE.

rohrschalmei. G. See SCHALMEI.

sackbut. A 32′ trombone. Named from medieval instrument.

sadt. A stop of gemshorn character. Named by Father Smith.[16]

salamine. An echo salicional.

salicional. (L. *salix*=a willow) I. salizionale. An open metal stop of string-like character. Small-scaled diapason.

salicit. An octave salicional.

sanftgedeckt. G. A gentle lieblichgedeckt.

saxophone. An old American imitative stop, either reed or flue, an open wood stop with harmonic bridges.

schalmei. G. Also schalmey. A reed imitative of the shawm, collective term for early double reeds. Equivalents for shawn are: G. pommer, bomhart, pumhart; F. bombarde. The schalmei was the highest member of its category.

scharf. G. D. scherp. A high-pitched or "sharp" mixture.

schnarrwerk. G. (*Schnarre*=rattle) A category of reed stops with short resonators of many varied shapes and sizes.

schweizerflöte. (G.=Swiss flute. Also schweizerpfeife.) Open flue, of gentle tone. A string-flute hybrid.

---

[13] Kinsky, *op. cit.,* p. 148.

[14] Sumner, *op. cit.,* p. 299.

[15] Irwin, *op. cit.,* p. 161.

[16] Sumner, *op. cit.,* p. 300.

schwiegel. G. Also schwägel. Flute "with truncated cones." [17] Possibly the obsolete "schwegel," a military fife.

septadecima. L, I. The seventeenth.

septième. F. Mutation, generally the flat twenty-first. Also 2 2/7' or, in pedal, 4 4/7'.

seraphon. Large flue on high pressure and having a wide mouth.

serpent. 16', 8'. A reed with tone between that of bassoon and trombone. Named from long instrument of the cornett family, curved to bring finger holes within reach of the player.

sesquialtera. Normally a two-rank mixture containing 2 2/3' and 1 3/5' ranks forming a sixth. Can be used (*a*) to form a cornet, (*b*) to add color to fluework, (*c*) or as a bridge between flue and reed stops.[18] In the Apostlekirche in Cologne a pedal sesquialtera 10 2/3' and 6 2/5' was built.

seventeenth. G. terz, F. tièrce, I. decima settima. Mutation of 1 3/5' (3 1/5' pedal, rarely 6 2/5'). A quiet diapason or gemshorn.

sifflöte. G. F. Sifflet. Small-scaled, open metal flue, usually 1' (or 2').

singengedeckt. 16', 8', 4'. Stopped wooden flue.

soave. I. A soft 8' stop.

sordun. F. sourdine, I. sordini. (1) A soft gedeckt. (2) Sometimes the sordun is a muted regal.[19]

spillflöte. G. Also spindelflöte. A quiet, metal flute, called "spindel" (G. and E.) due to the shape of its cylindrical tube mounted by an inverted cone.

spitzflöte. G. Also spireflöte. F. flûte à fuseau, flûte conique. Tapered metal flue with audible seventeenth. G. *spitz* means "pointed," and the stop has a somewhat pointed shape.

stentorphone. (Gk=loud voice) A loud, open 8' flue.

stillgedeckt. (G.=quiet gedeckt).

stopped diapason. E. F. bourdon; S. tapada, tapadillo. An 8' stopped flute, usually wood. See GEDECKT.

suabe flute. (=Swabian flute) A 4' wooden stop, open, quadrangular and with inverted mouths.

subbass. G. F. soubasse, sousbasse. I. subbasso. A pedal bourdon 32' or 16'.

subbourdon. See SUBBASS.

subprinzipal. G. F. principal bass. Open 32' pedal flue.

super octave. A fifteenth or doublette 2'.

sylvestrina. Stop made in Germany in early nineteenth century, somewhat stringy in tone. Willis used the name for flute-string hybrid stop.

tapadillo, tapado. S. See GEDECKT.

teneroon. (=tenor plus bassoon) Term used in nineteenth-century England to denote an incomplete stop.[20]

terpodion. (Gk.="to delight" plus "a song") A small-scaled, open metal flue having slightly reedy intonation.

tertian, terzian. D. tertiaan. A two-rank stop sounding the interval of a third,

---

[17] *Ibid.,* p. 300.

[18] *Ibid.,* p. 301.

[19] Irwin, *op. cit.,* p. 180.

[20] Sumner, *op. cit.,* p. 302.

e.g., in the 8′ series, 1 3/5′ and 1 1/3′. Earlier German examples had three ranks, e.g., 4′, 3 1/5′, and 2 2/3′.

tibia. (L.=a pipe) Flute, most examples of which are of broad tone and poor-blending quality.

tièrce. (F.=the third part) G. terz, D. tertiaan. The seventeenth, a mutation most commonly used at 1 3/5′ pitch, though in German organs also at 3 1/5′ or 6 2/5′ pitches.

traversflöte. G. I. flauto traverso. Stop imitative of orchestral flute tone.

tremulant, tremolo. A device for creating "a regularly recurring disturbance in the wind supply." [21] Used in Renaissance and baroque organs. Frequently used only for expressive passages of relatively soft level of tone, though some hair-raising examples of early usage with full combinations are to be found. As a special effect, it should be employed with reserve, as its effectiveness is in inverse proportion to the extent of its use.

trichterregal. (G.=funnel-reed) An old stop named from the shape of its resonator.

tromba. I. Reed stop of smooth character. It is loud and close toned but blends well.

trombone. Reed, commonly 16′ or 32′ in pedal, sometimes 8′ or 16′ in manual. Close toned. Invaluable pedal stop, especially for proper performance of early G. music.

trompette. F. Loud free reed.

trompette en chamade. Horizontal reeds, generally visible in the organ case. In Spanish organs placed in decorative, fan-like array.

trompette militaire. F. A free-toned reed made by H. Willis III to imitate French cavalry trumpets.[22]

trumpet. Reed used for chorus or solo purposes.

tuba. A loud stop of trumpet class. Sometimes as tuba mirabilis (L.=wonderful tuba), a loud stop best used for solo purposes.

tuba clarion. A 4′ tuba.

tubasson. A 16′ pedal trombone intended for solo purposes.

twelfth. A mutation stop, 2 2/3′. (1) Part of the diapason chorus, (2) flute (nasard) used for color, or (3) part of cornet formed from separate ranks.

twenty-second. 1′ stop, the third octave, most commonly found as part of a mixture.

unda maris. (L.=wave of the sea) A céleste. Two ranks, commonly dulciana, also flute, gamba. Occurs often as a single flat-tuned rank to match a similar regular-tuned rank in creating the céleste.

untersatz. G. Subbourdon or subbass.

vigesima nona. The twenty-ninth.

vigesima seconda. The twenty-second.

vigesima sesta. The twenty-sixth.

vigesima terza. The thirty-third.

viol, viole. Small-scaled open flue with beards, rollers, or bridges.

[21] Barnes, *op. cit.*, p. 104. The quotation comes from Stainer and is quoted by Barnes as being funny, which it is in an English sort of way.

[22] Sumner, *op. cit.*, p. 304.

viol céleste. F. Two ranks of string quality, one sharp tuned.

viola. Gamba, a string. Often of well-blending quality like the geigenprinzipal.

viola da gamba. I. String stop named from old Italian instrument.

viola d'amore. I. F. viole d'amour. 8′, 4′. A gentle string.

viole sourdine. Gentle string stop.

violetta. I. 4′ string stop.

violin. Open metal flue, imitative.

violin diapason. See GEIGEN.

violoncello, cello. I. F. violoncelle. Open flue, imitative.

violone. I. F. violon basse. Open flue, nonimitative string. A useful diapason-string hybrid.

vogelgesang. (G.=bird song) L. avicinium. A stop imitative of birds. Two or three small open pipes bent with tops immersed in water.[23]

voix céleste. F. L. vox coelestis. A mild string, two ranks, one of which is sharp tuned.

vox angelica. (L.=angelic voice) G. engelstimme. Refined céleste with a slow beat.

vox humana. (L=human voice) F. voix humaine, G. menschenstimme. Ancient stop of schnarrwerk class. Now a short-tubed clarinet-type stop with caps partially stopped. Used often with tremulant in chordal passages of romantic character. Also highly useful as solo voice in early music, especially when combined with such stops as nasard or nachthorn 4′.

waldflöte. G. (Wald=forest). L. tibia sylvestris. D. woudfluit. Open flute of 8′, 4′, 2′ (1′). Usually wood.

waldhorn. (G=forest horn) Reed of moderate power having smoother tone than the trumpet.

wienerflöte. (G.=Vienna flute) Open wood flue, delicately toned.

xylophone. A percussion stop, made with rosewood bars over metal resonators.

zartflöte. (G.=delicate flute) Soft hybrid flute. Later examples made as quintaton with harmonic bridges.[24]

zauberflöte. (G.=magic flute) A stopped, overblown flue with prominent twelfth.

zink, zinck, zinken. Reed, usually 2′ or 1′, named from ancient trumpet-like instrument.[25]

[23] *Ibid.,* p. 306.
[24] *Ibid.,* p. 307.
[25] See Kinsky, *op. cit.,* p. 96.

Index